Elizabeth Kim

Doubleday

New York London

Toronto Sydney

Auckland

Ten Thousand Sorrows

The Extraordinary

Journey of a Korean

War Orphan

PUBLISHED BY DOUBLEDAY
a division of Random House, Inc.
1540 Broadway, New York, New York 10036

DOUBLEDAY and the portrayal of an anchor with a dolphin are
trademarks of Doubleday, a division of Random House, Inc.

Book design by Dana Leigh Treglia

The names and identifying characteristics of some of the individuals
in this book have been changed to protect their privacy.

Library of Congress Cataloging-in-Publication Data

Kim, Elizabeth.
Ten thousand sorrows / Elizabeth Kim.—1st ed.
p.   cm.
1. Kim, Elizabeth.   2. Korean American women—Biography.   3. Korean
Americans—Biography.   4. Racially mixed people—United States—Biography.
5. Racially mixed children—Korea—Biography.   6. Orphans—Korea—Biography.
7. Women—Abuse of—Korea.   8. Seoul (Korea)—Biography.   9. California,
Southern—Biography.   10. Fundamentalism—Biography.   I. Title.
E184.K6 K44   2000
973′.04957′0092—dc21
[B]
99-052870

ISBN 0-385-49633-8

To Omma

I kiss your face a thousand times
Again, again, again.
I close your eyelids, smooth your hair
And fold your gentle hands.
Butterfly wings that beat
Against the domed ceiling of this life
Flutter free now in the open air.
And I will whisper this truth
Into the viewless winds:
I love you. I love you. I love you.

My heartfelt thanks to Gary Klien for the integrity of his fine writer's mind and the constancy of his support; to Catherine Hedgecock, Lawr Michaels, Paul Cannon, Gracie Doyle, and Stephen Calnan for their encouragement and loving counsel; to my agent, Patti Breitman, who believed in this book long before I did; to my editor at Doubleday, Amy Scheibe, for her insight and thoughtfulness; and to Dr. Roberta Seifert, for her wisdom and calm guidance on my journey through the darkness.

There is no way to fully express the depths of my love and admiration for my darling daughter. She saved my life and gave me a reason to live. She is the most brilliant and beautiful woman imaginable. Omma would have adored her.

Ten
Thousand
Sorrows

Prologue

I don't know how old I was when I watched my mother's murder, nor do I know how old I am today. There is no record of my birth, or of my name. There is no record of my mother's brief life. No certificate records her death at the hands of her brother and father in an "honor killing."

Section

I

....

This memory: the rustle of her gown.
This memory: the incense in her hair.
This memory: she lifts me off the ground
holds tight and swings me, laughing, through the air.
I rage inside the dark and call her name;
I hide inside the dark and close my eyes.
The winter of my life is frozen pain;
the longing for my mother never dies.

....

Chapter One

On the night Omma died, it seemed as if the Land of Morning Calm held its breath in disbelief at the horror visited upon its children. The gusty December wind stopped blowing and the bitter cold settled down, unmoving, in our little house. The air was thin and brittle.

Omma prepared a special dinner of bean curd in chili and garlic with our usual rice and kimchi, and quince tea. She was more animated than usual, and talked to me as if I were a grown woman and an equal, not her small child. Her crumpled silk skin looked feverish, and her eyes darted to and fro as she talked.

Omma told me that somewhere in the world it would be possible for me to become a person. She explained her Buddhist belief that life was made up of ten thousand joys and ten thousand sorrows, and all of them were stepping-stones to ultimate peace. She said nothing ever truly ended, not even life. Everything continued in a pattern of night to day, dark to light, death to rebirth. Omma said honor was found in following one's heart, not in other people's rules. She talked about power. It might be possible for a woman—even a nonperson—to have power, she said.

When dinner had been cleared away and the floor swept, Omma filled the large, blackened iron pot with water and put it on top of the heating pit until it was comfortably warm. She bathed me carefully and quickly so I wouldn't get cold, then dressed me in a clean *hanbok*, an ankle-length cotton skirt with a short, wrapped bodice. She brushed and braided my long, curly dark hair, which usually was covered with a white scarf. She handed me a folded piece of rice paper covered in fine writing and said that before first light the next day I was to leave the village by the dirt pathway, carrying the paper, until I found someone on the main road to show it to. Bewildered but accustomed to obedience, I simply nodded.

Omma grabbed me fiercely and crushed me to her body, pouring out a torrent of love in whispers. She told me over and over how precious I was, how beautiful and perfect. She told me she valued my life more than her own. She told me I was her beloved.

Omma released me and pushed me a few inches away, then told me to step inside the large, woven bamboo basket beside our bed, which we used for storage space. "Whatever happens, be absolutely silent, and remain here until just before first light," she said. Eyes fixed on her face, I obeyed silently, crouching down in the basket. Darkness descended as she closed the lid.

As the next hour or so wore on I sat cross-legged in the basket, watching the candle flame flickering through the slats of bamboo and seeing slivers of Omma as she sat motionless in front of the little wooden Buddha. Her sonorous chanting filled the room, the pure sound rising and falling. I waited, wide awake, tense and afraid.

The candle had burned low and the room was in twilight darkness when hurried steps outside sliced through the quiet, and voices filled the room. I was aware of a confused tangle of noise and movement and I pushed my face toward the slats, adjusting my view through the half-inch-wide gaps so I could better understand what was happening.

I recognized the voice of Omma's stern-faced father, a village elder who had never once spoken directly to me. I recognized the voice of Omma's elder brother, a loud young man who was an important village leader.

Both had done an unprecedented thing that afternoon: They walked up to Omma as she was working in the rice field and spoke to her. We were working quickly, trying to keep ourselves as warm as possible. I straightened up for a moment, aware that someone was coming, and was amazed to see my grandfather and uncle walking toward us. Since they were elders in the village, I knew this was a momentous occasion. Omma stood up, rubbed her tired back, then bowed and waited silently for them. The men did not bow but began speaking immediately in clipped tones. All three kept their voices low, so I didn't know what was being said, but I watched from a distance as they talked. All looked angry; my mother looked at the men with contempt. None of them bowed when the conversation was finished.

And now these men were crowded into our tiny home. With them was the young wife of Omma's brother. She didn't speak, and her head remained bowed. The men were wearing the high net hats that marked their importance as village leaders. Omma's father was a swarthy, barrel-chested man with a stern slit of a mouth and deeply etched lines down his cheeks. Her brother was taller and lighter-skinned. Omma's sister-in-law was wearing a stiffly starched white *hanbok*.

Omma's brother did all the talking. He told her the family had discussed the matter again since presenting demands to her that afternoon in the field, and he, his father, and his wife were there to carry out the plan. A family had offered to take the *honhyol*—me—into their home as a servant. They had seen me at work in the rice fields and decided I was now old enough to be useful around the house and also to be betrothed. The people making the offer planned to fill two needs at once: Add a servant to their home and find a future wife for a young man in their employ.

From the impassioned demands of Omma's brother, it appeared a sum of money had also been promised. Though they held respectable positions, our relatives were poor, as was everyone in the village, and the chance of reaping a financial windfall and ridding themselves of the family's shame—all in one move—must have seemed like an incredible piece of luck.

Omma remained kneeling before the altar. She didn't move a muscle, but her voice was steel.

She told the men that her feelings hadn't changed since the conversation in the fields, and that she would never sell her daughter into slavery.

Her brother told her that a female *honhyol* was already less than a slave, and elevating such a one to the status of a servant would be a move up in the world. He told her the family who wanted to buy the *honhyol* was respectable and the opportunity was more than either Omma or her nonperson child deserved.

Another thing her brother made clear in his didactic tone

was that the people who were making the offer insisted on Omma's approval, or no bargain would be struck. They were willing to buy a servant, but they were not willing to go against the wishes of the mother. Approving the transaction would go far in expunging the family's shame and also in reconciling Omma's family to her.

My mother didn't move from her kneeling position before the Buddha as she gave her final word. No matter what the offer might be or how badly the family wanted her to accept, it couldn't be done for one simple reason: Her child was gone. She told them that she had sent her daughter away to save her from the family's plan and that the child was in hiding where they'd never find her.

Omma's brother took two steps forward and slapped her with such force that she fell over and the small wooden Buddha toppled to the floor. Flecks of spit flew from his mouth as he told her she was filth, beyond all redemption, and that because of her unrepentance there was only one recourse left.

He yanked her off the floor by her hair and told his wife to tie Omma's hands and feet. Omma didn't resist, and kept her eyes closed, chanting under her breath to the compassionate Buddha. Her white *hanbok* was smudged with dirt, but the blue sash was still tied in perfect asymmetrical neatness across her chest. Her hair had come loose from its twist and tumbled down her back in a pure, shining stream.

In the bamboo basket, I fought to keep my breathing still, as my teeth met through my lower lip and the blood poured down my chin.

Over the strong, age-blackened beam in the corner of the room, grandfather threw a rope. He said nothing, and kept his lips pressed tightly together. The two men worked quickly, fashioning a noose and slipping it over Omma's bowed head. As they pulled the rope taut, my mother rose in the air until all I could see through the bamboo slats were her bare feet, dangling in midair. I watched those milk-white feet twitch, almost with the rhythm of the *Hwagwan-mu* dance, and then grow still. They seemed to stretch, the toes pointing straight down to earth as if she was going to pirouette on their tips.

I didn't realize that I had stepped out of the bamboo basket. I was unaware of the tears and blood dripping off my face. I could see nothing but my beloved Omma suspended between heaven and earth. I ran to the white, limp feet and covered them with kisses. I called for my mother until I had no breath left.

I remembered the others in the room only when I felt rough hands grab me and pin me down on the altar. Her brother cursed and said that even when facing death, Omma lied to them. And now, he said, they had to deal with the evil thing she left behind. He ordered his wife to hold my arms still, and his father did the same with my legs. His father had not spoken at all; his wife spoke for the first and last time in that place, asking the men to spare my life and promising she would get rid of me the next day. Her husband spat before replying. He reminded her that I was nothing—not a person, and not worth any feelings.

He ripped off my clean *hanbok*, grabbed the matches from the altar, and lit the first one. He forced my legs apart and held the flame to my flesh.

The agony was so intense it blotted out thought and left nothing but pinwheels of white fire in my view.

Chapter Two

In the Confucian village where I lived with Omma, filial piety was the supreme virtue. Ancestor worship was a way of life, and obedience to elders was absolute and unquestioned. To rebel against the word of an elder was to invite social censure of enormous magnitude. Women were at the very bottom of the hierarchy and existed only to serve men and to give birth to men. Their voices were supposed to be soft; their eyes downcast; their spirits quiescent. Their role was not to think but merely to obey. To disobey a male relative—especially an older one—was unthinkable.

In that clearly ordered world, I believe, Omma was a problem from her childhood on. She rejected Confucianism, announcing she had converted to Buddhism. But she really crossed the line of disobedience when she told her parents she wanted no part of an arranged marriage—something most Korean women simply accepted.

The few times she talked about herself to me, Omma made it clear that she had done nothing for which she was ashamed. She was a free, creative spirit who struggled for expression. Her restless mind must have seemed threatening and dangerous to her family and neighbors. Her dreams didn't come true, but she was true to them. She didn't berate herself for anything in her life, she simply accepted the way the wheel of fate had turned.

I absorbed my mother's sense of acceptance and spent most of my life believing that everything that happened simply was the way it was supposed to be, for good or ill. To rail against fate was senseless; the only thing to do was accept what one was given in life.

But as she was growing up she enraged the village elders and shocked the women with her rebellious ways and heretical ideas. Her grim-faced father beat her and her shrill mother screamed at her, but nothing changed her. Inside she seethed and schemed and planned her escape. Her family reminded her again and again of her duties as a daughter, and threatened her with the most dire of consequences: complete estrangement from the family and the village. If she brought dishonor on the family, she would be considered dead to them—not a daughter any more, not even a person. The threat was made daily, and Omma shrugged her graceful shoulders and continued to work in the rice paddies.

In her gentle way, she was a rebel. She longed for the city, for electric lights, for laughter and conversation. She chafed against the narrow confines of her life. And always, lit from within with the glow of hope, she dreamed of love.

In that strict Confucian culture, girls remained with their mothers until they were married and then became like slaves to their mothers-in-law. Women waited their entire lives for their mothers-in-law to die and their sons to marry, so they could dominate someone else and continue that mindless cycle of cruelty.

A woman was irrevocably dishonored if she committed any of the *chilgo chiak*, or seven evils:

> Disobeying her in-laws
> Bearing no son
> Sexual looseness
> Being jealous
> Carrying a hereditary disease
> Talking too much
> Stealing

Men had no such rules.

Eventually Omma ran away from her home and went to Seoul. She wanted to be a singer. Her high voice quavered expertly over the Korean five-note scale, and in her dreams she was a *kisaeng* of old, entertaining the nobility and astonishing everyone with her talent and beauty. In those dreams she left the village—and its suffocating patriarchal rules and dull complacency—far behind.

When the chance came, she didn't hesitate. Somehow, perhaps from her work in the rice fields, she had finally saved enough money for the train ride. So long before dawn she packed her good *hanbok* dress and a few other necessities in a neatly tied square of cloth and headed down the worn path that led away from the village.

Seoul was immense. But Omma was not easily intimidated, and she soon found work and a small circle of acquaintances. In the humble noodle house where she dished up bowls of *naeng myon* in cold broth, she became friends with a regular customer. He was from America, a place that seemed as remote as the moon. In broken Korean, supplemented with a dictionary, he told her about his family, his home, and his duties as a soldier. He gave her a tiny American flag and told her it meant that where he lived, everyone was free. He played jazz records for her. And he knew far more about her land than she did. He told her about the recent armistice that ended the Korean War and divided the country.

To Omma, starved for knowledge and conversation, he was without equal. She was fascinated, and soon she was in love. Like so many other women of her age and station, my mother hoped that this soldier would be different from others: He'd keep her with him, even in America; he'd never leave her.

But he did leave, and Omma's quick, high-arched step became slow and shuffling; her lilting voice became hoarse and dull; and soon her body became unwieldy. When it was obvious she was with child, she lost her job and had no prospect of getting another one. There was only one thing to do: return to the village, carrying in front of her the unmistakable badge of her shame.

She was oblivious to everything but the magnitude of her loss, the inconsolability of abandonment. Nothing her father or the village could say or do would hurt her; every fiber of her being was already unadulterated pain.

She was pregnant, carrying a GI's child. She was destitute

and desperate. She had been nothing when she left the village; she was less than nothing now. A nonperson carrying a nonperson, without hope and bowed down with shame.

On the day of Omma's return to the village, most of its inhabitants were out in the fields. She walked into a hut she knew to be empty on the outskirts of the village—no one wanted to live there because it was remote and cramped—and began cleaning it up. She was beyond caring what would happen; all she wanted to do was rest. When people returned from the day's work, word spread quickly that the village's firebrand was back.

But while no one offered hostility at first, no one offered welcome either. She was tolerated but not embraced. Her family wouldn't visit her. Whatever friends she may have had couldn't risk the disgrace of being seen with her. From that moment on, she remained on the periphery of village life. No one said anything when she quietly returned to her old place in the rice field. No one spoke to her at all.

I don't know how Omma managed when the time came for my birth. Perhaps the village midwife decided to ignore Omma's dishonorable status in return for payment. Perhaps Omma was left to her own devices. At any rate, I was born healthy. Omma now had a child and an ally. Now there was someone who didn't care about her status or her past sins. There was someone who needed her, loved her, and wanted to spend every moment with her.

Probably within a few days after my birth, Omma was back in the rice fields. There was no long period of convalescence, no doting relatives to pamper her. She bundled me up in a cotton sling carried against her chest and went back to work.

I was her constant companion, and when I got old enough I worked by her side. We earned just enough rice for us to eat and to trade to take care of our most basic needs.

From time to time we stopped our work and stretched our aching backs, hands on hips, shoulders shrugging and releasing, fingers flexing. From the fields we could see the village in the distance, looking small and insubstantial against the austere beauty of the mountains.

The village existed for one purpose: to grow rice. Everyone depended on each other to get the job done. The rice field served the whole village and beyond, and everything centered around it. It was the lifeblood of the people there: for food to eat, for food to sell, for the basic necessities of life such as coal for the heating pits and tea and medicinal herbs.

The tiny village was breathtaking in its beauty: a verdant, lush valley on the outskirts of Seoul, surrounded by Korea's million mountains. Visually, it was the embodiment of Korea's name: Land of Morning Calm.

Around us were misty mountain peaks; spread out at our feet were riotous fields of cosmos, azalea, and ginkgo. Tender shoots of rice stood like tiny emerald spears in their shimmering beds.

Chapter Three

I was a small, dark-haired girl walking hand in hand with my Omma down the dusty road from the rice fields back to our small cottage. The top of my head came about to her waist, and as we walked along I looked up repeatedly to catch a glimpse of one of her tiny, brief smiles. It was a journey we made every day, after hours of standing barefoot in the soggy fields where we planted, tended, and harvested the precious rice.

When we were alone on the road, Omma let me stop to add to my frothy bouquet of lavender and red cosmos, which would be arranged in a ceramic kimchi pot and put on our tiny altar.

At dusk, with the mountains rising ahead of us, we trudged on tired feet, mine dragging as I tried to keep up with Omma. She stared straight ahead, her head wrapped in a white scarf, her *hanbok* dress muddied. I was her shadow, staying close beside her, keeping my face as expressionless as hers. The air was crisp and stinging, and I looked forward to the *ondol*—the small heating pit—which was used both to keep our cottage warm and to cook the rice for our meals.

Out of the corner of my eye, I saw movement. Several people stood outside one of the nearby cottages, raising tea bowls to their lips after their long day's work. The cups stopped midway. The casual chatter was stilled. There was silence, then I heard the spitting begin. I was the first to be hit by a pebble; I felt it sting me in the back, below my shoulder blade. I didn't cry, nor did I look behind me. Omma did not shield me. We said nothing. She squeezed my hand tighter and we walked on, a little more quickly but still staring straight ahead, without any show of weakness. The next pebble hit me on the cheek, then a volley struck us both: back, arms, legs, and faces.

The catcalls began: "*honhyol,*" a despicable name that meant nonperson, mixed race, animal. After each insult, the rock-throwers would spit, as if to cleanse their mouths of the word.

Once we passed the village proper, the rocks no longer reached us. We walked to our one-room home, on the outskirts of the village at the end of the long dirt road, away from all the others. The mountains, purple before the setting sun, loomed ahead. We kept our eyes on them and our backs straight, walking without hesitation or misstep, until we were inside. Once safe behind our door, Omma caught me up in her arms and cradled me against her chest. She wiped the blood from my cheek and gently rubbed my bruised back, but said nothing about what had just happened.

Bundled up, we made our dinner and took it outside, where we sat on the far side of our tiny house, the rest of the village blocked from our view. We sipped scalding tea and ate our hot rice and spicy radish and cabbage kimchi from ceramic bowls, as we watched the purple mountains turn to black.

With my mother, a small bowl of rice lasted for many minutes, because we ate slowly, with ceremony. Omma ladled out the rice, then placed the bowl in both hands and bowed to me. I bowed back and accepted the bowl, and we sat facing each other, taking slow bites of the rice and then savoring the fragments of spicy kimchi. Augmented with sips of hot barley tea, meals with my mother were emotional banquets.

She would wait courteously for me to take the first bite, and often she'd pick up an especially crisp morsel of white cabbage from the kimchi bowl with her chopsticks and pop it in my mouth. Sometimes I tried to feed her, but I wasn't as skillful with chopsticks as my graceful mother. Nevertheless, she smiled at me and ate whatever I gave her.

....

We ran that gauntlet on the dusty road over and over. My mother never spoke of it. She never raised an arm to deflect the rocks, nor did she shield my small body with her own. It wouldn't have occurred to me to ask. As I look back, I believe she knew her death was approaching. She knew she wouldn't be there to protect me. She knew the price she paid for giving birth to—and then keeping—a child with tainted blood.

And while she thought of herself as a rebel from her culture, in a very Korean manner she prepared me the only way she knew: She stayed beside me and shared my pain, but she forced me to face the situation with her and to do it with my head held high and no tears on my cheeks.

Omma never tried to comfort me by saying I was equal to the others. She never said the problem was everyone else. In fact, I think she believed I was not equal to others. Omma accepted that I was a nonperson and that we were outcasts, but she loved me anyway. We were like two lepers living in a tiny colony of our own—we knew we were diseased and couldn't mix with the rest of the world, but we created a tiny haven of peace for ourselves.

In Asian culture, in which bloodline and honor are immensely important, there has historically been an intolerance for mixed-race children. National pride is deeply ingrained, and in Korea the intense love for the country's heritage and traditions has its darker side of hatred for anything that taints the purity of that heritage.

I don't remember feeling any resentment that Omma didn't shield me from the rocks, nor do I remember feeling resentment that no one shielded me from the rocks that came as I got older. Having known nothing else, I just felt like that was the way it was supposed to be.

•   ....

Omma was a serious woman. Once, I believe, she had been spirited and mischievous. Faint traces of that girl could still be seen from time to time, but only when we were alone and playing or dancing together. She was in her early twenties, but there were lines around her eyes and her shoulders were bent.

I rarely saw Omma smile, but when we stood together in the rice field her tight mouth relaxed and her forehead smoothed as she watched me work beside her. When we walked through the field, my feet stuck in the squelching mud as I struggled to work as quickly and as smoothly as my agile mother. Omma stopped from time to time to help me along and to adjust my scarf and hide my curly hair. But there was no disguising my face. I could see Omma tremble when we were out in daylight together; I could see the speculative looks of passersby sharpen into contemptuous recognition as they realized what I was.

Omma was beautiful, at least in my eyes. She had a waterfall of straight black hair that grazed her hips and skin like slightly crumpled silk. She had a beautiful mouth, with delicately curved lips. Her forehead was high and her nose small and finely molded. Omma's hands were strong and calloused, but she used them with the utmost gentleness. She smelled like woodsmoke and the incense she burned in the evenings. She was tall in comparison with other women in the village, and unlike many of them she stood up very straight. Her bearing was gallant.

Omma's hair was straight; mine was curly. My nose was a little bigger than hers, my eyes a little rounder. My skin was the same tanned ochre.

She had great reverence for the natural world, and she taught me about the magnificent plants that grew wild in our land, the forsythia and rose of Sharon and the sacred lotus. We loved them almost as much as we loved the mountains that watched over us night and day.

In the evenings we sat outside our one-room house and watched the mountains in silence. Sometimes we sat side by side, but most often I nestled between her knees and she held me lightly, rocking back and forth as we gazed on the mountains. I learned meditation in her gentle arms, without a word of teaching being spoken.

I was a fairly quiet, introspective child. Omma taught me everything she could, from gardening and cooking to music and storytelling. When it was time to cook the rice, Omma measured it in her hand and then let me measure it in mine. When she checked to see if it was done, she tasted a grain and then had me taste one. When tasting the kimchi to see if it was seasoned correctly she watched me test it, chewing and nodding seriously if I thought it had enough red pepper.

We had a small garden outside, where we raised radishes and green onions and potatoes and cabbages and cucumbers.

Our tiny home had packed-mud walls, a thatched roof, and a neatly swept earth floor. In the corners were strong wooden beams. It was one room—a peasant's home, able to stand against the elements, with nothing superfluous. There, when the evening rice and kimchi had been eaten and the bowls cleaned, we knelt before the wooden altar and chanted to the Buddha of Mercy and Compassion.

The small wooden Buddha was one of the few things Omma brought back with her from Seoul, and it was precious to her. Before she began to chant, Omma's preparations were simple: She took off her shoes and washed her face and hands.

I watched Omma chant and thought that no one in the world could be as beautiful. Her satin hair was freed from the scarf that she wore in the fields, and it flowed down her back. I loved Omma's hair. I would run my fingers through it, looping and playing with it. I sometimes came up behind her when she was kneeling at the altar and silently tucked my head beneath the curtain of her black hair, pressing myself against her back and feeling her hair tumble down over my own shoulders and my own back.

Omma never scolded me for interrupting her meditation, but neither did she leave her place at the altar. She continued to chant or sit in silent meditation, sometimes smiling at me and gently shaking her head, kneeling with her back straight and her tiny feet just visible beneath the hem of her *hanbok*.

Omma rarely let her hair fall free; most often she twisted it and put it up on her head, holding it in place with a deft turn and a single polished sliver of wood. Her movements were spare and graceful and achingly beautiful. I sat on the bed and watched her as she lifted her arms, the *hanbok* sleeves falling away from her fragile wrists, to put up her hair. Tendrils escaped first, then the whole heavy mass began to slide, and she put it up again, over and over.

In the evenings, if she wasn't too tired, Omma sang "Arirang" and the other folk songs I loved, and we danced together. She taught me that a true musician relies on *hung*—her inner inspiration—rather than on a prescribed formula, so I stood in one corner of the room and concentrated, my eyes shut tight. When I felt the *hung* stir inside my small body, the bleak room and dirt floor vanished. Then in our imaginations we clutched our heavy satin skirts and twirled across the endless marble floor in *Hwagwan-mu*, the Flower-Crown Dance, with our crowns balanced perfectly on our sleek, perfumed heads. All around us, music pulsed and the air was sweet with night-blooming jasmine. And finally, breathless, we collapsed in a tangle on the bed, wearing our threadbare cotton *hanboks*, back once again in the room with its dirt floor and bare walls, our hair flying and the air around us thick with dust.

In her sweet, high warble, Omma sang:

> *Arirang, Arirang, O Arirang,*
> *The pass of Arirang is long and arduous,*
> *But you will climb to the hilltop,*
> *Where the sun will always shine.*

Arirang, Arirang, O Arirang,
The times in which we live are most trying,
To this thousand miles of river and mountains
May peace and prosperity come.

Omma made only a few dishes, but they were delicious. Her kimchi was a work of art. She set cabbage to soak overnight in salt water, then rinsed it three times the following day. In massive ceramic pots she layered the cabbage with slivered scallions, radish, garlic, and ginger. Over that she poured salt, water, and a palmful of powerful red peppers. To release the air, she poked around in the mixture with chopsticks, then covered the containers and weighed them down with rocks. We buried them in the backyard until the vegetables fermented and were ready to eat.

The result was glorious.

I don't recall ever eating meat with Omma—and I don't know whether that was because we were too poor to buy the beef that Koreans love or whether she chose vegetarianism for her own reasons.

Besides kimchi and rice, Omma sometimes made a spicy cucumber salad with the requisite red chili peppers, vinegar, garlic, and green onions, and a soup with bean threads and green onions—and whatever other vegetables happened to be available at the time: maybe mushrooms or carrots or green peppers.

In our house there were three pieces of furniture.

The wooden altar, which we polished every day, held a tiny statue of Buddha and a picture without a frame, propped against a rock. In the picture was a young, smiling man wearing a uniform. I had never seen anyone with clothing like that, or whose hair and eyes were so light. We never talked about the picture, but sometimes late at night I woke up and saw Omma kneeling before the altar, rocking gently back and forth, cupping the picture in her hands.

Across from the altar was our bed. She kept me between the wall and her own body, protecting me as best she could from the cold night air. At night we slept, snuggled tightly together, nestled in precarious warmth in our little cocoon, while the cold wind howled outside.

Beside the bed I shared with Omma was the large bamboo basket in which we kept our treasures: a special *hanbok* she bought in Seoul before my birth; a tiny piece of silk with red, white, and blue patterns that she called "the stars and stripes"; and my precious cardboard village and stick people.

Omma had created an entire world for me with some old boxes and a few sticks. The sticks she whittled and polished and decorated with bits of cloth. The two primary characters were a mother and daughter, but there were friends and neighbors, all with permanent, happy smiles painted on their faces and colorful *hanboks* and trousers made out of scrap cotton. The cardboard buildings were all different: a palace with large windows, cozy cottages, and a Buddhist temple. In our little play town, no one was sad or lonely. People came every day to visit our mother and daughter, and the entire village gathered at their home for meals and dances.

On the ground behind our house Omma made mountains for the toy village: She covered mounds of dirt with tiny twigs— creating a pine-covered slope—and tiny petals represented fields of wildflowers. Sometimes the stick mother and child went for journeys over the mountain, and each time the entire stick village gathered for a farewell party. There was another party when the two returned, and our little creations entertained their friends and neighbors with wonderful tales of the magical lands over the mountains.

In that little cardboard world I was queen. Anything was possible. The stick people reenacted *Ch'uinbyang-ga*, in which a girl from the country finds her Prince Charming in Seoul; and they danced in the dirt to *Salp'uri*, freeing their spirits from trouble and anguish.

From Omma I learned folk stories that were handed down, I'm sure, from her parents and their parents before them. Unlike Western folk stories, there was never a "moral" to the tale—at least none that Omma told me. The only meaning a story had was the one you chose to take from it.

My favorite was the story of the good brothers:

Two brothers once lived who loved each other dearly. They took care of each other and divided everything down the middle.

After harvest they put their rice in sacks, and the older brother thought, "My younger brother just got married, so he has a lot to worry about. I'm going to put an extra sack of rice in his storeroom without telling him, because he probably wouldn't accept it and I'm sure he needs it more than me."

That night he tiptoed into his brother's storeroom and put the sack there.

But the next day Older Brother found the same number of sacks of rice in his house that he'd had before. He couldn't understand it, but decided to just take the sack of rice back to his brother's house. He did, and the next morning was amazed to see the same number of sacks in his house as before.

Now he was really confused, but he decided to try one more time. It was a full moon, and as he walked along the path he saw someone coming toward him, carrying something on his back. It was Younger Brother, carrying a sack of rice. They saw each other and began laughing, finally understanding why the number of

*sacks stayed the same. Younger Brother had been bringing an extra
sack to Older Brother, because he loved him so much.*

....

We were poor, but I never knew it. Omma's imagination created
palaces to dance in and different dresses of silk and brocade for
us to wear every night. We had little food, but I didn't know I
was hungry. With Omma, a bowl of rice was a banquet. We were
locked in isolation, but I wasn't lonely. In Omma I had mother,
storyteller, playmate, confidante, and defender.

On mornings that we weren't working we sometimes went to
the market to buy tea and spices and vegetables. Everyone was
out and about on those mornings, doing their shopping, gossip-
ing with friends, washing the laundry. No one in the village itself spoke to us, but with the gentle courtesy that never deserted
her, Omma continued to bow—and taught me to do the same—
whenever we met someone. Sometimes, on the narrow dirt pathway, we came face to face with members of Omma's family.
Without speaking or making eye contact, they pushed by as we
left the path to give them room. And always, my mother bowed
deeply, her body eloquent with love and grief. If they ever noticed, they made no sign, and Omma waited until they were
gone before she straightened up and took my hand again.

Without passing any judgment on their behavior, Omma had
told me who everyone in the village was. I knew my relationship
to each person we saw in the fields and on the path, and the fact
that my *haraboji*—grandfather—and my other relatives took no
notice of me concerned me very little.

In the evenings, when the others gossiped together and
drank tea after the day's work in the rice paddies, we stayed on

the outskirts of the village circle, sitting outside our own little home and playing our own little games. Omma told stories of a wonderful world beyond the mountains, where there was always enough food and it was warm all winter long and there was nothing to fear. "Someday you'll leave this village," Omma told me. "Someday you'll be a fine lady and everyone will speak to you and smile at you."

"And you'll be with me, Omma," I answered, looking eagerly into the beautiful, beloved face. She didn't reply, but gathered me in her arms and held me tightly, covering my dusty face with soft butterfly kisses.

Chapter Four

I don't remember much of the night after Omma's death. It must have been several hours later before conscious thought reasserted itself, and I was aware of being huddled in a corner of our house, whimpering. My buttocks and vulva were in excruciating pain from the burns. Omma's body was gone. My relatives were busy packing up our few belongings, and none of them spoke to me or even looked in my direction. I was dazed with misery, but I knew enough to keep as silent as possible.

In a while my grandfather and uncle left the house, carrying the basket and a couple of bundles. My aunt put me into a wagon and set off down the dirt pathway, pulling it behind her. The wagon jostled me painfully, but I dozed off and on until we arrived at an orphanage on the outskirts of Seoul.

"She has no name," my aunt told the orphanage official. "I don't know her birth date or how old she is. She's nobody. She was left to die by her mother, who committed suicide, and we found her." In the orphanage I was given some first-aid salve and clean strips of cloth to cover the burned flesh, but no one spoke of my wounds.

It was an old, familiar story in that post–Korean War society: A girl brings disgrace on her family by having a child out of wedlock and by an American soldier, and after a few years she can't bear the dishonor and isolation of being an outcast and kills herself. Mixed-blood children were often mistreated by people who hated them because of their tainted heritage. Many were abandoned by their mothers and either entered a life of slavery or lived on the streets, begging or stealing for food. The people at the orphanage had seen it all, and neither my physical condition nor the story told by my aunt was anything new.

Being nameless was just one factor in my shame. Names are so important in Korean culture that the family often consults fortune-tellers before naming a child. A child's name can shape the future, because it brings good or bad luck with it. The Korean family is based on the male family line, and the family register contains the names of paternal ancestors for over five hundred years.

Being without a birth date added another level of shame. A Korean's fortune depends in large part on *saju*—the year, month, day, and time of birth. An auspicious combination of the four can mean a charmed life.

In a Korean's view, it would be better to be dead than to be the embodiment of shame such as I was: a *honhyol*, a female, nameless, without a birth date.

My mother had, in my recollection, only called me Sooni, her own private pet name for me. The derivation was the Korean diminutive for "little girl"—an appellation for a dearly loved, small child. I didn't tell the people at the orphanage that, nor did I tell them what had really happened the night before. I remained silent, too lost in despair and too schooled in obedience to speak.

During the long trip from my home to the orphanage, my aunt had not spoken to me. She had interceded with her husband the night before to spare my life, but I don't know why the decision was made to let me go to an orphanage. And if the villagers doubted the story my family told—that a young woman, overcome at last with the magnitude of her own sins, hanged herself and left her daughter to die—none of them did anything about it.

A woman's life had little value anyway, so removing it for the greater good of expunging a family's shame was a long-accepted practice. Such deaths were not murder, they were honor killings, and therefore sanctified by tradition.

The orphanage was run by Christian missionaries, so it was there I was given my first taste of Western religion. The children were kept in slatted cribs, one on top of another, four to a stack. The cribs looked much like animal cages at a shelter—four deep and lining three walls of that large, stark room. In all, there were probably twenty of them. They had latches on the outside that let the outer square of slats drop down, but they couldn't be opened from inside.

I was accustomed to a great deal of physical freedom—days

spent working outside in the rice paddies or playing in the fields beyond our house. The only time I'd been confined to a small space was when I watched from the bamboo basket as my mother was killed. The crib was terrifying—not only because it was too small for me to move around much but mainly because I wasn't able to get in or out of my own free will. Another person had control over my movements—a violation of the human spirit I had never experienced before.

The walls of the room were white and dotted here and there with pictures of Jesus. The surfaces were all washable, the linoleum floor bare. I sat hunched in my cage—a kindergarten-size child much too big for the baby-size space—in a bewildered haze of misery. When anguish overcame me I slammed my head against the slats and screamed and pulled my hair until someone came by and told me to be quiet. Except for accidental contact, I don't remember ever being touched in the orphanage.

Directly across from my cage was the door. I sat, hour after hour, with my eyes focused on the crack around three sides of the door where the light could be seen. Sometimes the light dimmed for a moment and then I knew that someone was about to open the door and come in. I held my breath, waiting for the door to swing in and a human being to stand directly across from me. I waited desperately for whatever faces came into my view.

Beside the door was a roll-top desk, its top scarred and dull. Inside were bundles of papers. I was fascinated and terrified by that desk. From time to time a woman sat down there and pulled out a bundle of papers, then shuffled through and made marks on them with a pen. Almost immediately after, one of the children would be gone. I didn't know then that the bundles were adoption papers, but I knew they connected in some way with the children there. I wondered if I was contained in that desk also, and if someday my bundle would be marked on and I'd disappear.

For years, well into my adult life, I had recurring nightmares about that desk. I'd be walking past it, barefoot on a cold, hard floor. I'd hear a sound like wind rushing through a tunnel and feel a magnetic force sucking me inside. I'd be pulled, helpless, underneath the scarred roll-top and into the cubbyholes where the papers were stashed. I'd find myself in a room with a dirt floor, strapped to a table, and people would be standing around branding ugly names on my body with hot irons.

In the orphanage, I watched people walk by and kept a non-stop fantasy running in my head: I pretended I could reach out through the slats and grab them and pull them to me and make them open the door and speak to me and look in my face.

Sitting in the cage, nails dug deep into my skin, I tried to ameliorate grief by increasing my physical pain. And just below the awareness of that misery, breathing rhythmically like a monster waiting to devour me, was the knowledge that it was because of me Omma died. My face and my dishonorable blood had killed the only person I loved and the only person who loved me.

The orphanage was overcrowded and understaffed, and there was no comfort to be found there. Everyone was an island of their own private misery. Every child was given one blanket, and it was supposed to be kept clean and provide sufficient warmth. Everyone was cold. All the blankets were dirty. The mattress in my crib was old, cracked plastic that made crunching sounds when I moved. It was covered in a cotton sheet patterned in faded orange flowers. The crib was too small for me to stretch out completely, so I either stayed curled up in a fetal position or sat hunched.

There was a surfeit of suffering, and one person's story was no worse than another's. There was the tiny girl, about two, who had been found tied up by some people who were scavenging in a trash can. She was terribly emaciated and cried incessantly.

There was the newborn baby, still with umbilical cord intact, dumped on the front porch. Because the cribs were all filled, he was given some rudimentary medical care and then placed in the cage with me. I was told to watch him. I was terrified for him. They had wrapped him in one blanket, but I was afraid it wouldn't be enough to keep a baby warm, so I put mine over him as well. Then I just sat, pressed against the slats, hugging my knees with my arms, and watched him throughout the night. I was so afraid that I might hurt him if I moved or fell asleep. I felt a huge weight of responsibility and longing for this tiny life.

The next morning I realized that despite my intentions, I'd dropped off to sleep in the night. I lifted the blanket and touched the baby's face. It was bluish and cold. I unwrapped the blanket and touched his arms, his feet, his bloated blood-encrusted stomach. I knew even before the adult came by to check on him that he was dead.

I wept over and over for that baby. I never knew where he came from, but I thought of him as mine. He was unwanted and nameless, like me. He was completely helpless and at the mercy of others, like me. I felt as if saving his life would somehow atone for not being able to save my mother's life. And when he died I was sure it was because of something I did or didn't do. Maybe putting an extra blanket on him made him too hot. Maybe lifting the blanket in the morning to look at him made him too cold.

....

Aside from crying—which could be heard just about all the time coming from one or more of the cribs—the orphanage was pretty silent. People didn't talk to each other; no music played.

There were a few children in the orphanage about my age, but most were younger; many were babies. All of us had physical characteristics that branded us: curly or light hair, hazel irises or round eyes. Each a *honhyol*, but taking no comfort from the others. Despite the fact that we lived in such close proximity, we never really got to know each other. I didn't play with the other children or even talk to them much. We were all locked in our own little miserable worlds, and we sensed the competition between us. Without really knowing what the orphanage's purpose was or what adoption was, I knew I was vying with the others for the approval of whatever adults might visit. I knew sometimes visitors liked a child so much that they took her away.

From time to time people walked through and examined the orphans, either as prospective parents or as go-betweens lining up a child for someone else to adopt. Those visits were torture. I held my breath, willing visitors to stop at my cage and open the door. I tried to look pleasant and docile. But people walked on past, usually going to a younger child. We had visitors every few days. If you were a childless couple and you didn't mind having an Asian son or daughter, Korea was fertile ground at that time. There were so many forgotten children, the product of brief liaisons between soldiers on their way through and women on their way to hell.

The one photo taken of me in the orphanage shows a bleak-faced girl with dank hair, skin swollen and blotched from crying. My adoptive mother later said I looked like a drowned rat. The woman who was in charge told me to smile; otherwise no one would ever adopt me. Nobody wants a grumpy little girl.

One couple came in several times and divided their attention between me and another, younger girl. She was about two, cute and friendly. Finally one day the couple came in and took the little girl with them, leaving me behind. The woman in charge of the orphanage told me they chose her because she was young, and I was too old; she was pretty, and I was ugly.

The belief that I was too old and too ugly continued throughout my life. I was sure that anyone I dated would leave me in a second for someone younger, someone more desirable. I felt inferior to any younger woman. It didn't matter that I was more intelligent, wittier, or whatever: The mere fact that she was younger imbued her with power that I didn't have. Ironically, as I got into my thirties the men who were attracted to me got younger. Most of my friends have usually been a decade or two younger, and they never seemed to give it a second thought. I always worried, though, that they were just being kind to the older woman in the group. No matter what age I was, I always felt too old.

Every day in the orphanage we followed pretty much the same routine. We were awakened early in the morning and our blankets were taken out to be shaken and aired. The best moment of the day for me was when the cage door was opened in the morning. I climbed out and went to the communal bathroom, jockeying with all the others to be first in line to use one of the few toilets. After that we all had to wash our faces and hands quickly in basins of cold water.

The orphanage had one large room, which was lined with the cages. At mealtimes tables and chairs were brought in and set up down the middle of the room. We all sat in the same places each mealtime. Everyone got a bowl of rice, sometimes with a few vegetables mixed in.

I got more food to eat in the orphanage than I had with Omma, but it wasn't as satisfying. No longer were mealtimes gracious rituals in which my mother chose the best morsels for me and we gazed at each other while we shared our rice and kimchi. No longer was my tea handed to me with a smile and a bow. In the orphanage a bowl of rice lasted a few seconds, because everyone tried to eat as quickly as possible.

We stayed at the tables after breakfast, and after they cleared away the dishes the missionaries taught us a few Christian songs, like "Jesus Loves Me," and told us some Bible stories. The songs and stories were an odd mix of English and Korean, since the orphanage workers were American missionaries who had learned the rudiments of my language. But since the whole point was to get the children adopted—and a knowledge of English would make us more desirable—they taught us English words when we had no idea what they meant. So I sang "Jeeza raub me, dees ahno" without having the faintest idea what I was singing.

Then, depending on the weather, we were sometimes allowed to go outside for a while. There was no playground, but there were a few toys scattered across a large lot. On the days we went outside I stayed on the far side of the building, nearest the mountains. I sat in the dirt and played with sticks, looking up every few seconds at the bluish-gray mountains in the distance.

The sight of the mountains was the only comfort I had in that place. When I felt the panic and anguish well up in my chest, I looked up at the mountains and felt a slight easing of the pressure under my breastbone. On days we stayed inside I sat as close to the window as possible—everyone else wanted near the window too—because a tiny sliver of mountain was visible from the inside.

The missionaries never encouraged us to do much; there were no organized games or crafts. Except for the religious teachings, the children were pretty much left to their own devices or shut in their cribs to be out of the way.

Most of the time, I thought about Omma. I didn't talk much

to the other children in the orphanage, but I kept up a running conversation in my mind with my mother. I made up the kind of stories she made up: ones where we traveled to the other side of the mountains and found wonderful worlds there. In the afternoons we were given a snack—usually crackers or something else that didn't require dishes—then put back in the cages for nap time and let out again at dinner—more rice and vegetables, usually with kimchi added.

At night before bed we had another Bible story and listened to a prayer. I liked the story of the birth of Jesus, because it reminded me of Omma's story about how the world began: Hwanung, son of the divine creator, descended from heaven and was looking over his domain when he heard the prayer of a bear who wanted to become human.

So Hwanung gave the bear garlic and mugwort, and the bear later became the first human woman. That woman then prayed for a son and became pregnant—without the help of a man—giving birth to Tan'gun, Korea's founder. Since neither one had earthly fathers and both were all-powerful, I wondered if Jesus and Tan'gun were perhaps related, but the missionaries told me that was impossible: Jesus was the real Son of God and Tan'gun was just a myth. One was a biblical truth; the other was heathen ignorance.

All the children there were to become Christians whether we liked it or not. It didn't matter to me one way or another. I was willing to do anything necessary to keep the peace, to find some measure of kindness and acceptance. If Jesus would help get me out of the orphanage, then I'd believe in Him.

And in time, I grew to find the thought of Jesus very comforting. He seemed so gentle, for one thing. The pictures of Him on the orphanage walls were lovely—tenderly holding a lamb, spotless white robe gleaming, looking from the painting directly into my eyes. When I got older I got in the habit of whispering His name when I awakened from the horrific nightmares that came every night. I pictured Him scooping me up just like the lamb in the picture and protecting me from all harm. I said it over and over in the night, as a talisman against evil and darkness and grief: "Jesus. Jesus. Jesus."

....

One of my torments in the orphanage—and indeed throughout my life—was that I had absolutely nothing of my mother's. Omma's sister-in-law had let me take nothing away from our home, and so I sat and thought with longing of my wonderful stick people and the cardboard village Omma had made, the little wooden Buddha and Omma's beautiful *hanbok*, and even the picture of the American man.

I was frantic for something she had touched, something she had cherished. And since arriving at the orphanage and being washed with disinfectant, I couldn't even smell her scent on my skin.

My grief was boundless, but my rage was directed at one person: me. There were two things I believed: My life was a terrible mistake, and I deserved nothing but suffering. My hatred of myself, born at my mother's death and nourished in the orphanage, grew with each passing year.

So I lay curled up in a fetal position in my crib and began a nearly lifelong pattern of digging my nails into my skin. I pressed against the flesh of my upper arms or legs or neck until there was a sharp explosion of pain and, with it, a small sense of release of my guilt and anguish. That was the only way I knew to vent the boiler room of agony in my heart.

....

In the orphanage I tried to stay awake as much as possible. Sleep was the enemy. I waited inside my cage for salvation, and I knew that if I fell asleep and salvation came, it would pass me by.

So I sat in my threadbare maroon cotton trousers and shirt, knees pulled up to my body and arms wrapped around my knees, and stared through the bars. My long curly hair, which Omma had loved, was cropped short by the large, silent woman who handed us our food every day and gave us the burning antiseptic baths that were supposed to kill any lingering parasites. I sat and hugged my knees and ached and waited. Whenever someone walked through to examine the children I smiled and smiled. My fear was that I might fall asleep and the someone who was going to rescue me would walk through the room. If my eyes were closed, they wouldn't be able to see me.

Months passed before it was my turn to leave the orphanage, but it didn't happen the way I'd fantasized. My new parents, a missionary couple, had made all the arrangements without ever having seen me. One day I was simply led into an office, where a tall Caucasian man—a representative of the adoption agency—was waiting, and a few minutes later we were gone. The actual day of my release was anticlimactic. For so long I'd waited and waited, watching the door across from my cage and willing someone to walk in and take me away, and when it finally happened it was all over within a moment. I simply felt numb.

There was no record of my age, so a birth date was chosen by an official at the orphanage—the month and day I entered the orphanage. Someone looked at my teeth and estimated the year of my birth. I had no personal possessions, no family records, no name. I had no identity at all except for what my new parents chose to give me.

....

It was spring in Korea, and the wildflowers were blooming in intoxicating profusion. The valley was lush and green; the beloved purple mountains in the distance were still capped with melting snow. It was the time of year in which Omma and I would have been outdoors as much as possible, playing with our make-believe village and picking fresh bouquets every day to place beside Buddha on our little altar.

On the day of my departure I was given a cotton dress, bordered in red and white checks, and ankle socks. Those clothes, which like my maroon trousers and shirt came from castoffs sent to us by American churches, felt uncomfortable and alien. The dress was too big. I wore green rubber shoes with tiny red flowers painted on them, and I had pictures of my new parents in my hand. I had been taught a few words, including "Mom" and "Dad," and all I knew was that those words connected with the strange people in the pictures.

The orphanage director told me I was going far away to a wonderful place called America and would live there forever with a nice family. She told me to never forget how lucky I was.

I had lived my life with Omma in the midst of rice paddies and wild azalea fields and Korea's million mountains on all sides. I had never seen a car or television; when it got dark we went to sleep and at first light another day of work began. Our meals were a shared bowl of rice and the kimchi we buried in ceramic pots. It would be twenty years before I again tasted kimchi.

The entertainment Omma devised for us was our dances and stories and long periods of quiet, looking at the mountains together. I had no concept of what an airplane was, but now I was going to get on one and fly to some unknown place where no one would speak my language, where rice and kimchi and quiet were unheard of.

I had always believed that when I traveled over the mountains to the magical lands Omma described, she would be there with me. Without her, I didn't much care what was to come.

Chapter Five

The trip from Korea to America was a pleasant change from the orphanage. The man from the adoption agency accompanied me, and for the first time since my mother's death I was alone with an adult who paid attention to me and pampered me.

Someone was finally speaking directly to me, breaking the silence I had lived in and making me feel as though I was no longer invisible. He knew the basics: words for hungry, thirsty, bathroom. I could say *"mul"* and he handed me a glass of water. I could say *"pyonso"* and he took me to the toilet.

On the day of my trip to America,

we took a taxi to the airport and boarded the plane. I was so tired, so bewildered and relieved to be out of the orphanage that I wasn't afraid of the huge metal bird or the strange people milling about. It all had a surreal quality, like a dream. It was so alien that it wasn't frightening. My new friend smiled at me often and carried me most of the time. I held on to his coat lapel as if he were my lifeline. But although he was kind and considerate, he was to become the conduit between one life of confusion and loneliness and another.

When we got on the airplane the stewardess tried to put me in the seat next to him, but I cried and clutched him and the two of them said something in English to each other. She smiled and he smiled, and I got to sit on his lap until I felt brave enough to stretch out in the next seat. We got little meals on trays, which I found fascinating. He gave me his pocket watch and a white linen handkerchief to play with. I unscrewed the glass cover and watched the tiny hands click around the dial, and wrapped the clock up in the handkerchief. That gold-plated pocket watch kept me content for a few hours. He slept part of the time, and I slept; and he read a magazine and I played with the watch, and thus passed a few hours of limbo between misery and misery.

Our flight stopped in Hawaii for a few hours, and he took me to a little store near the airport. There, for the first time in my life, I was given something brand-new, something that had been bought just for me.

He bought me a small troupe of fuzzy animals: a mother tiger and her three cubs and a mother and baby penguin. Each one fit in the palm of my hand. The tigers were gold and black, with white velvet throats. They were linked together with black silk ribbon. The penguins were black and white, with red felt mouths in Cupid's bow smiles. The flippers of the mother and baby were joined at the tips, as if they were holding hands. They

44

were the most amazing and beautiful things I'd ever seen. The mothers and their children couldn't be separated from each other unless they were wrenched apart, which I had no intention of ever doing. I tucked the smallest of the tiger cubs into the curve between the mother tiger's paws, because I knew that nestling against Omma's chest was the most wonderful place in the world to be.

The weather was clear and warm in Hawaii, and I felt something almost approaching peace. Someone other than my mother was treating me kindly. It didn't matter that he couldn't speak much of my language; he was gentle and smiling. I started to feel safe again. I had known him for only a couple of days, but already he was the only familiar thing in an increasingly unfamiliar landscape. On the flight from Hawaii to Los Angeles, I played with the animals. I had stopped wondering what would happen next in my life; it was enough just to be out of the orphanage, out of the cage, with someone I liked. I wondered if maybe I could stay with this person, and I was relatively content.

But then we landed in Los Angeles. We got off the plane and he walked across the wide, shiny floor of the airport with me in his arms. I watched, amazed and apprehensive, as people rushed around me. Their shoes clacked on the tile, their voices swirled in a garbled tongue that I didn't understand. Later when I learned the Bible's story of the Tower of Babel, I thought back on the airport and wondered if it sounded like that.

Toward us came two people: a man and a woman. They talked loudly and smiled and looked at me, and I clutched tighter to his coat, pushing my face against the stiff white cotton of his shirt.

I was afraid of the woman, because she was wearing two dead animals around her shoulders. I saw a bushy-tailed red fox draped around her with its pretty face gaping lifeless over her bosom and the tail of a twin fox stuffed into its mouth. I was especially horrified by the eyes of the foxes, which were wide open and staring. The eyes were glass, I learned later. The woman wore high-heeled shoes that clacked against the airport floor, and her light-brown hair was puffed out into a shiny cloud. She was smiling broadly, shouting incessantly at me as if I'd understand her language if she were loud enough.

The man with her was tall and slim, wearing a black suit and white shirt. He didn't say much, and after a few minutes I was unceremoniously shoved into his arms. My friend walked away without looking back over his shoulder, while I screamed and tried to wriggle away so I could follow him. My new father held me tightly and sat down on an airport chair until my tantrum subsided.

The person I had started to trust was handing me over to these people, without explanation or comfort. I wondered why I was being left again—why my friend, who seemed to like me, was giving me to strangers.

In the years that followed, I never forgot him. Once I let him into my heart—even in just the few hours it took—he remained there. I never saw him again, but when I grew up I began following his career, which was quite illustrious. I often thought about writing him, but I assumed he wouldn't remember me and I was afraid of embarrassing him or humiliating myself. I didn't really want to try for a renewal of our strange friendship, but there were some things I wanted to tell him. I wanted to thank him for making me feel alive again. I wanted to thank him for looking into my eyes and smiling—he was the first person to do so since my mother's death. In his presence I wasn't a nonperson or a burden or an unadoptable orphan; I was a human being. I wanted to thank him for buying me something and trusting me with his pocket watch and treating me gently. I wanted to thank him for carrying me in his arms. I wanted to tell him that the memory of the few hours we spent together is very precious to me and that his understated, circumspect kindness had a lasting effect on my life.

I think that any loving act, even if it's only momentary, has a limitless power for good. A big part of the reason I feel that way is the memory I have of him.

For many years I wondered why he handed me off in the abrupt way he did, but now I think it was probably the only thing he knew to do. And taking himself out of the picture as quickly as possible was probably what he was trained to do when bringing an orphan and new parents together.

As I was sitting in the airport, sobbing, a girl walked over and tried to give me a piece of chewing gum. Beyond comfort and rational thought, I slapped away her hand as she held out the gum. My new parents were horrified and scolded me loudly. Just a few minutes into my life in America I began to feel my first pangs of regret. I didn't know what they were saying, but I certainly knew they were angry. I felt bad for hurting the little girl's feelings too, and I couldn't communicate that to her.

Those moments in the airport set the stage for my future life with my parents. In my mind, Mom was some kind of monster who decorated herself with dead things. Dad was quietly disapproving. I was an ungrateful person who didn't behave properly.

In a few short months I had gone from talking only with Omma to this noisy place with many people speaking a language I had no hope of understanding. I was utterly bewildered. My new parents couldn't help—they had learned no Korean, not even "yes" or "no." They called me by a new name. They scolded me for crying. There was nothing familiar in this new, alien landscape.

While my parents sat in the front seat of the car, talking with each other, I cried myself to sleep on the way home from the air-port. I didn't wake until a few hours later when we pulled into the driveway of my new home.

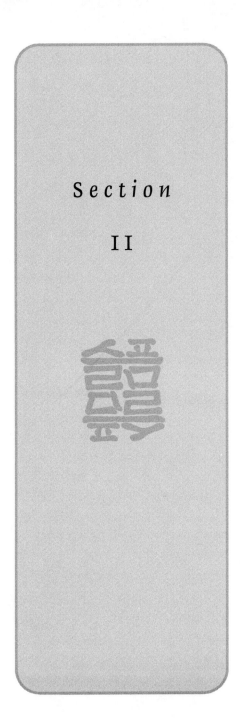

Section

II

....

It's time to die now.
It's time to close the door.
It's time to steel yourself
and say good-bye
and never cry
again.
It's time to die now.
It's time to clean the house.
It's time to bathe yourself
and bid farewell
to earth and hell
tonight.
It's time to die now.
It's time to give up pain.
It's time to grant your wish
for no more tears
or dark or fears
or life.

....

Chapter Six

I awoke in the desert, a kind of place
I would never have imagined could
exist. Outside was a vast stretch of
dead, sandy ground. There were
no wild azalea fields or rice paddies. There were mountains, but
they were dry and barren. Instead
of pine-studded slopes curving up
into misty cloud banks, I saw grace-
less piles of rock. There were no
ginkgo trees. There were no sacred
lotuses. There were grayish man-
zanita bushes and unforgiving needle plants called cholla.

The wild creatures in the area
had adapted to living in hell. There
were scorpions that skittered across

the burning asphalt driveway. There were vinegaroons that hid in dark recesses, then gave out a painful sting and a vinegary smell. There were coyotes, worn down to gaunt muscle and bone, that came down from the hills at dusk to eat somebody's pet or a wild jackrabbit. Snakes undulated from one bush to the next, leaving their curvy imprints all over the sand. Science fiction–sized spiders built their enormous webs in the wooden eaves above the kitchen door. In the cracks between fenceposts were brown recluse spiders with bites containing a poison that would eat away inches of soft tissue.

The air felt as though it was pumped out of a giant oven, with occasional blasts of even hotter wind that picked up the dirt and created miniature whirlwinds with it, sandblasting whatever was outside. There was no grass. No true green existed in that wasteland.

In front of the house were wide white steps leading up to the front door. Dad carried me to the front door and then put me down, and I looked in amazement at my feet, which were on something soft and furry—I learned later it was called "carpet"—that I was afraid to step on. In front of me I saw an enormous black box on three slender legs. I had no idea that it was a piano, or that I'd be spending a good part of my life in front of it in the years to come. Off to the side was a red velvet sofa, and beyond that a door that led out to the dry, tumbleweed-strewn backyard.

That modest house was overwhelming to me, with its stretches of beige shag carpet and large, important pieces of furniture. Down the hall from the living room were three bedrooms and a pink-tiled bathroom. My new parents took me into my room to show me my new toys and my bed. The bed was four-poster walnut, covered in a yellow chenille bedspread with a huge daisy in the center. I was given a stuffed tiger, a black cat,

54

and a pink doll with a plastic face. They told me later that I showed no appreciation or enthusiasm, and they were disappointed in my lack of manners.

I'd never slept in a bed before and wasn't sure what to make of this huge thing. I didn't realize that the room and the toys were for me.

My fear grew moment by moment. In Korea I had experienced alienation, and grief, and loss, and loneliness—but this fear was something new. I didn't know what was coming next, and no one could explain anything to me. Everything I saw and heard and tasted was completely unfamiliar.

I looked at everything and said nothing. I had learned in the airport that these two people couldn't understand me, and I couldn't understand them, so there was no point in trying to communicate.

After a quick tour of the house, my new mother immediately began molding me into her image of a perfect child. She took off the green rubber shoes and the faded cotton dress I was wearing and gave me a pale-blue dress with two rows of ruffles and a scratchy underskirt. The Korean Airlines bag that held my little troupe of animals was pried out of my hands. Later, when I could understand enough English, she explained to me that the animals were unhygienic and had to be thrown away. But by that time I was too exhausted to cry any more. I was resigned to the knowledge that anything I held dear would be summarily destroyed.

I crawled underneath the piano, taking with me one of the immaculate new stuffed animals from my immaculate new bedroom, and pressed myself against the wall. Even with my budding claustrophobia, that spot seemed the safest place in a house that was huge and confusing after my one-room home with Omma and my locked crib at the orphanage.

At dinnertime I was tugged out from under the piano and taken into the dining room, where fried chicken and mashed potatoes were laid out. I knew it was food, but the look and smell were alien and nauseating to me. My parents scolded and tried to push bits of food in my mouth, which I kept resolutely closed. I wanted some rice. I wanted tea. I wanted them to shut up and quit jabbering incomprehensible words at me.

By that time, I think, they were pretty exhausted themselves, and we all went to bed. I don't remember anything more about that night, except that I woke up several times and stood on my bed and looked over the headboard, peering into the two-inch space between the wood and the wall. I was afraid of that space and what might come out of it during the night.

On my second day in America I came to a decision: I was going to understand these people and their strange ways. By now I connected them to the photographs I'd been given in the orphanage, and I assumed that I was going to stay with them until they got tired of me or until I made them so angry that they returned me to the orphanage. I lay awake in bed and looked at my new bedroom, thinking it all over. I didn't think this new relationship was permanent, any more than any in the past had been, and I believed that whether they kept me or threw me away depended on how I acted and looked.

I had learned, first in Korea and now in America, that I was unacceptable. I thought that if I tried very hard, maybe I could modify the way I looked or sounded enough to please those around me.

At breakfast on day two I tried to eat the egg and bacon on my plate. I knew what eggs were, but I'd never seen bacon. The soft-boiled egg was slimy and gelatinous, and I gagged on the first bite. The bacon was the saltiest thing I'd ever tasted, even saltier than kimchi. My new parents had definite ideas about

56

what foods belonged with what meals, and I ate a breakfast of fried eggs and bacon every morning while I lived with them. I never liked it. I tried to mimic the way my parents held their forks, which I'd used a few times at the orphanage. The best part of breakfast was the orange juice, which was poured from a big plastic pitcher into a tiny fluted glass. It was so fresh and sweet and clean. I drank it in a few gulps and looked longingly at the pitcher, wishing I could have more. Even if I could have spoken English, I wouldn't have asked for anything, and I learned later that you ate and drank what you'd been given. Nobody at that table ever got more orange juice.

What I had known was lost, and my life became something completely foreign. *"Mul"* became "water." *"Pyonso"* became "bathroom." I became "Elizabeth," a girl I did not yet know how to be. "Omma" was never replaced. All that was left was a void where that word had been.

My training—to become the Elizabeth they wanted—began immediately and was relentless. Every moment was monitored; every word and action and thought were scrutinized in the light of my parents' standards and the Bible's dictates, and usually I was found wanting.

I had already had a little exposure to Christianity during my time at the orphanage, but what I'd seen was just the tip of the iceberg. I knew about blessings before meals, but the interminably long prayers I heard from Dad were something new. Mealtime prayers in my new home were an itemized list of everything on the table, a catalogue and repentance of all the sins of the day up to that point, a request for health and well-being for everyone who was sick, and a lament about the lax political and moral climate of the time.

I was beginning to understand my parents, little by little. I felt the least uncomfortable with my new dad, who didn't talk as incessantly and didn't stare at me. After breakfast on that second day I took his hand and pulled him all over the house, pointing to each item. He understood pretty quickly what I wanted and said the name of each thing twice, until I repeated it, nodded, and moved on. He held my hand nicely—not too tight, but securely—and I started to like him. I pointed to myself and to him and to the sky and the grass and pictures of things in books— everything I could think of. The naming process took the greater part of the day.

I fell asleep in midafternoon and napped under the piano, in what was to become a favorite spot. From there I could watch my parents' feet coming and going, and I had a wall at my back, which made me feel a little more secure. I listened intently to my parents as they spoke and began trying out words and inflections, whispering to myself. They seemed pleased with me— Mom clapped her hands when I pointed to her and said "mother." I was heartened with that small show of approval, and wondered if maybe I could make my new parents happy.

When I woke up from my nap under the piano, I felt dizzy and sick to my stomach. I crawled out, walked over to the red velvet sofa, and vomited worms all over its cushions. I hadn't yet been to see a doctor and I carried parasites in my body—most likely from the unsanitary conditions at the orphanage. I don't know why I chose the sofa—I don't remember having time to make a conscious choice. Mom screamed and Dad grabbed my arm and yanked me away from the sofa. I knew I had just done something awful, and I felt ashamed and afraid. They shouted at me for several minutes while I stood in the middle of the living room, feeling desperately sick, crying and shaking. There were a few words I recognized from my language lessons with Dad: "sofa" and "animal."

My parents cleaned up; I continued to stand where I was. I

didn't know what to do. Eventually Dad grabbed my shoulder and pushed me into the bathroom, where Mom was running a hot bath. The night before I had gone to bed shortly after dinner, and this was my first experience with a bathtub. In Korea I had bathed with Omma by heating water and pouring it into a small wooden washtub. Although the orphanage had a large bathroom with flush toilets, we were bathed simply by being sponged down from time to time with disinfectant.

What I saw in the bathroom was a huge white bowl, big enough to swallow me, with steaming water gushing out of a little silver mouth. I looked up at Dad and said *"anyo, anyo, anyo"* (no, no, no) over and over. Mom pulled off my dress and they pushed me into the tub. I tried to stay on my feet, but I fell several times and slipped under the hot water. I thought I was fighting for my life. As we struggled my parents and the bathroom got drenched, and at one point Dad slapped my face. The water was terrifyingly hot and deep, and I thought it was punishment for the worms.

After a few minutes Dad pulled me out of the tub and pushed me to Mom, who dried me off. I stood naked and shivering in the bathroom while they scolded me and mopped up the floor and walls with towels. Then Mom put my nightgown on me and said "bed."

....

For years after the worm incident, I apologized over and over, each time Mom talked about it. She said countless times that I was "just like an animal" when they first got me, and throwing up worms on a lovely velvet sofa proved it. I felt guilty and ashamed about it, and while Mom never said she blamed me for having worms, she said a person would have to do something disgusting like sit on the dirt without underwear to get them. But what she said most often was that she couldn't understand why, in a house with a nice bathroom, I had to throw them up on her sofa.

Mom was obsessed with that event. She told everyone she knew about it; she used it as an anecdote when she met someone for the first time. "So nice to meet you. This is my daughter, Elizabeth. She's adopted, you know. Oh, we had quite a time with her in the beginning. She was just like an animal. In fact, a few days after we got her she walked over to my lovely red velvet sofa and threw up worms right on it. Can you imagine? Well, it's never been the same since, of course. I just couldn't believe my eyes. They were wriggling all over the place. And the bathroom was only a few steps down the hall. Why on earth she chose to leave her worms on the sofa is beyond me. Have you ever heard of such a thing?"

The person she was talking to at the time would listen politely, disconcerted and embarrassed. They'd glance at me every few minutes while I stood quietly beside Mom. I always thought they were looking at me with loathing and that the disgust I saw on their faces was because of me. But now, as I look back, I think most people were disgusted with her. I think the glances they gave me were compassionate and that if they felt any horror at hearing the story, it was that she chose to recount it. I do remember everyone changing the subject as quickly as they could.

Mom's implication was always that my own mother and my Korean culture had been so barbaric that I was infested with parasites. But my mother, my Omma, hadn't let that happen to me. It wasn't the lack of Western culture that made me sick but the American orphanage and its filthy conditions. The white Christian missionaries, who had supposedly saved me, were to blame for my illness. It was their ill-treatment I was purging.

That event—and Mom's endless retelling of it—was a major factor in setting my self-loathing in stone. I believed that whatever was inside me, whether spiritual or corporeal, was disgusting. Recently my daughter told me how often Mom—her grandmother—told that story as she was growing up. Each time, Leigh said, she watched me carefully. "Your face changed," she said. "You looked desolate. Then you got very quiet and remote."

....

In the house where we lived, the walls were covered with pictures. The living room had prints of well-known religious paintings: Jesus standing before a garden gate, knocking; a reproduction of Dürer's "Praying Hands"; and one of an old man bowing his head in prayer before eating his meager slice of bread. As you left the living room and walked down the hallway, the pictures got more sinister: Jesus standing before Pilate just before His crucifixion; His walk to Golgotha carrying the cross. Right outside my bedroom door was a picture that showed Christ's eyes turned up in agony as the crown of thorns pressed on His forehead. The eyes followed you as you passed by.

On the wall above my bed was a triptych by Hieronymus Bosch, an artist who lived in the late Middle Ages. It depicted the Last Judgment. In the left-hand panel was paradise, where a few people walked in a green valley. Even in paradise, though, an angel was in the background, waving a sword at someone who evidently didn't belong there. In the middle panel was the judgment itself, with Christ on His throne surrounded by saints and angels. On the ground were all sorts of horrors: a half-duck, half-man creature carried someone hog-tied to a post, skewered through the chest with a long sword. A man's head floated in a barrel, while a green dragon stood ready to eat it. A fat man sat at a table, as red demons poured something down his throat from a large cask. Bodies disappeared into spike-studded grinders. Disembodied heads moved around on wheels. In the right-hand panel of the triptych, hell was depicted. Spurts of flames rose from craters in the ground. Naked women were fondled by gargoyles; the unholy had daggers thrust into their genitals. Creatures pecked away at the bodies of the damned.

Bosch and my parents had a lot in common. They were moralists who believed humans are inherently evil and if left to their own devices will end up in hell.

The house was dark, because Mom didn't want the sun to fade the massive old pieces of mahogany furniture. The double-thick drapes were kept closed, day and night. The house was crammed full of objects—religious pictures and books, china ornaments, Dresden dolls, and hundreds of other tiny, breakable things that had to be handled gently and dusted weekly.

The piano was draped in a silk fringed shawl. On the piano, and on just about every other flat surface, was a bouquet of plastic roses. There were crystal candy dishes scattered throughout the house, but none of them contained any candy. The house was sterile in its perfection, and I was afraid to touch anything.

....

On day three Dad began my piano lessons. By that time I could understand their language pretty well, and I knew what the piano was because Dad played it every day. He came home that night with what I called "piano book" for me. There were pieces in it like "Kitten on the Keys" and "Indian Brave." I was ambivalent about the piano, but I wanted to please Dad. The first lesson was the C scale. I watched Dad tuck his thumb under his third finger as he played the scale and tried to imitate his move, but my hands were half the size of his and my fingering was fumbled. Dad, who was trained as a professional pianist, was impatient with me, and each lesson was misery. I had an hour of lessons in the morning, before he went to work, and usually they ended with him storming out of the room, angry over my ineptitude.

"Why can't you play a simple scale? I've shown you over and over."

I told him my fingers wouldn't reach.

"That's ridiculous. Just stretch your hand. You're not trying. Why are you so bad?"

I had a hard time understanding classical music. I was fascinated with the grand piano and its ivory keys, but I was confused by Western music. My ears were attuned to Omma's five-note Korean scale and this new scale was intimidating. I was afraid to admit just how little I understood, so I faked a lot of it by watching Dad and imitating what he did at the piano. Once in a while I told him I didn't understand the music theory he was trying to teach me.

"Of course you understand it. You're not trying. You're just a bad girl."

I was told that music was for the glory of God. So when I failed I disappointed not only Dad but God as well.

I showed an aptitude for music that helped me sometimes avoid Dad's anger by mastering what he taught without understanding it. I could mimic without understanding a music, a language, and a life that was not my own. If I felt a sense of loss of the self I had known, I wasn't aware of it. I didn't want to remain the old Korean me. All I wanted was to fit in, to be accepted in this new world.

One evening during my first week in America a woman came to the front door of my parents' house carrying a box with two kittens inside. She said they were for me, because I must be lonely and she thought they'd cheer me up. She was a member of my parents' church, a round, jolly woman who laughed a lot. Mom and Dad smiled at her and thanked her, and I sat on the floor in front of the box. The kittens were gray and white, a little on the serious side, just like me. I scooped them into my lap where they sniffed around and purred and cried a little bit. I was entranced by them. I stroked them and cuddled them and whispered to them. "Be very, very gentle with them," the woman told me. "They're just babies."

I nodded my head. I knew about being gentle. I knew I wouldn't hurt them. The woman laughed and said we should take a picture of me with my new pets, so we all trooped outside. I gathered the kittens up in the skirt of the cotton dress I was wearing and followed the adults onto the patio. Dad brought out the camera and I squatted on the ground, my hands cupped around the kittens, with their paws on my legs.

They were so cute and so soft, and I stayed out in the backyard with them until the woman left. She came outside and stroked them, then gave me a big hug and told me to have fun with them. Once she left, things changed. Mom told me kittens were unsanitary and a lot of work. She said she didn't know if I was responsible enough to take care of them. Then she looked at my hand. The kittens had scratched me while we were playing, and Mom took me inside where she dabbed iodine on my hand and lectured me about diseases that cats carry. I hadn't noticed the scratches at all, but the tincture burned enough to make me cry. I asked her if I could go back outside with the kittens, but she said I'd played enough with them for one day and it was high time I went to bed. She and Dad began talking in low voices.

In the morning I ran outside to see the kittens, but they were gone, along with their box. I asked my parents where they were and they told me they sent them away. "Your hand got scratched. We might have to take you to a doctor now. No kittens for you."

Once again the lesson was clear: Anything I loved was taken away without my consent or understanding, just like Omma, just like my little troupe of toy animals. There was no warning given before and no comfort after.

In my new household, it was not only a shameful thing to cry or to feel fear, it was an absolute sin. Those emotions are of the devil, my parents said, because they show a lack of faith in God. Apparently any kind of emotion other than the Joy of the Lord was tantamount to blasphemy. When I was punished for something bad—giving mother an "ugly" look, using a "snotty tone of voice," not doing my chores properly—my primary concern was to keep the tears away. Sometimes I couldn't quite make it, and my lips began trembling. "Don't you make that face at me!" my parents said, and my quivering mouth got slapped.

After a while it got easier. I learned to swallow hard, until the tears and rage and grief formed a tight ball in the base of my throat. At some point it became impossible to cry. I simply couldn't do it. On the few occasions over the years when a tear or two escaped, the physical pain was frightening.

My parents were always devising ways to help me overcome my fears and learn to trust in God. For example, they had a little exercise for me to conquer my uncontrollable fear of the dark. At the end of the long hallway was my room. On the floor they placed my stuffed tiger. The hallway was dark; my parents and I were standing in the living room. "Now go down the hall and get your tiger," they told me, "and stop this foolishness." I needed tiger, but I was afraid of the dark hallway and what might be waiting in my dark room. They refused to turn on the light or walk with me, because, as they told me, they were trying to teach me something for my own good. Finally, after a long period of tears and pleading, I steeled myself to walk down the hallway, because I couldn't stand to think of tiger alone in the dark.

The house where we lived felt malignant to me. The light switch for the dark stairwell was at the foot of the basement stairs, for some reason, and often in the evenings Mom sent me down there to get soap or toilet paper or just check to make sure everything was locked up. I hated going down in the dark, but the return trip was worse. I stood at the foot of the stairs, my finger on the light switch, and coordinated my movements so I could dash up the stairs as soon as the light was off. "Slow down and walk up the stairs properly," Mother told me. "You're acting like some wild banshee. Now go back down there and come up like a lady."

So I walked back down the stairs with measured steps and a blank face. I stopped at the bottom, turned the light on and off, and walked back up. "That was too fast. And you're shaking. This kind of fear is absolutely sinful. What must the Lord think? Now you go down there and do it again. And this time smile as you're walking up the stairs. Remember, every little thing we do, even if it's just fetching soap from the basement, must be done to the glory of God."

....

One afternoon shortly after my arrival in America, I walked out of my new home and wandered across the street. I wanted to take a better look at the scraggly wildflowers and weeds growing in a vacant lot there, and I picked a few to make a bouquet for

Mom. She was taking a nap and Dad was at work, and I was bored and lonely. So I just opened the door and left. I thought it would make her like me more; Omma, after all, had loved the bouquets I picked for her in the fields around our home, and they stood next to Buddha himself on our little altar.

I was only gone a few minutes, at least by my reckoning. But when I walked in the front door Mom was on the phone to Dad, and I heard her say "Well, finally. Here she is." She put down the phone and stood with her hands on her hips.

It was quiet where we stood in the front hallway, with just the grandfather clock ticking. Mom's white dress was sprinkled with red poppies, her back was straight, her hair smooth. I was hot and dirty, with dust on my black patent-leather shoes and lace-trimmed socks. She looked at me for a moment, while I stood just inside the door, the glaring sun hitting my back and the wilting bouquet starting to shake in my hand. "And just where do you think you've been, young lady? Your father is having to leave work early because of you. I'll let you tell him what a bad girl you are when he gets home."

I didn't offer her the flowers, and she yanked them out of my hand and threw them away. "Don't bring weeds in the house. I'm allergic to these things. Are you trying to make me sick?" When Dad got home we all sat down in the living room and my parents catalogued my sins: stealing plants from somebody else's property, going outside without permission, worrying Mom. "Why are you such a bad girl? What are we going to do with you?" I got a severe spanking—the first one of my life. Dad held my upper body in a headlock, facing away from him, then slapped my bottom and legs with a wooden board. Worse than the physical pain was the fear of this new, unknown punishment. I didn't know spankings came to an end after twelve or so strikes; I didn't know what would come next.

Nevertheless, I decided it was nothing more than I deserved. I knew I was bad; I believed the adults around me. My life in Korea had taught me abject humility. And since I didn't understand yet what was bad and what wasn't, I was terrified.

That night, after I was put to bed, I crept out of my room and down the hall, just to sit outside my parents' bedroom door. I was still scared of the dark, and I felt afraid and alone. I wondered if they were going to send me back to the orphanage. I knew I wasn't supposed to call out for them in the night, but I thought I'd sit very quietly and just listen to their voices. I wanted to know there was someone else in the world with me. I heard Dad speaking: "I think adopting her was a big mistake." I tiptoed back to bed and stared at the ceiling, digging my nails into my skin.

Digging my nails into my flesh was the one way I found to distract myself from the anguish of my emotions, and I kept it up for many years. I never was comforted by the sensation of physical pain and the warm trickle of blood, but it gave me something else to think about. It also gave me a sense of expiation for the unbearable burden of guilt and shame I felt. Hurting myself somehow satisfied my desire for justice.

As I got older I often dug my nails into my neck until I created a red, scabbed welt around the entire circumference of my throat. I dug my nails into the soft hollows around my eyes. I often awoke in the night to find myself curled up in bed, in a fetal position, with tears streaming from my closed eyes and my nails embedded in some vulnerable spot. I would awaken and realize I'd been digging my nails into my vagina. Sometimes in those awakenings I'd whisper, "It's time to die now. It's time to die now." Nearly every morning there was blood on the sheets and dried blood on my skin.

My parents never seemed to notice; or if they did they were

too embarrassed to say anything. And within a few months after my arrival I began doing all the laundry, so I was the only one who had to deal with the bloodied sheets.

Looking back, I'm amazed at how adaptable and eager to please I was. I learned fairly fluent English in less than a week; how to play the piano in less than a month; and how to behave like the proper Christian daughter they wanted almost over-night. I was willing to do anything to win their approval. I desperately wanted to deserve their love.

Chapter Seven

After a few days in America I learned to smile. I smiled so much it hurt. And if I forgot, Mom looked blankly around the room and said, "Hmmm. I hear a voice but I can't see anyone. I imagine that if some little girl would smile, I'd be able to see her." So I'd stretch my lips wide and beam madly at her, and then she'd acknowledge my presence.

That little game was symbolic of life in that household: If I didn't look and act the way my parents wanted, I didn't exist. If I wasn't smiling, Mom said that "Big Chief Storm Cloud" had managed to sneak in the room and must leave immediately. And my smile had to be big enough and sunny enough to make Mom say "Oh, there's a nice little girl. I think we'll let her stay."

I was invisible if I didn't do exactly as they wanted. I began to believe that if I didn't become the perfect child, I'd disappear.

I wanted desperately to fit in, to be the same as the people around me. When Dad stood in front of the mirror, adjusting his tie or fixing his hat before going off to work, I stood beside him and compared our faces. "I look just like you," I said, as my ochre skin and dark curly hair and almond eyes were reflected beside his tall, all-American fairness.

I hated the way I looked. Whether in Korea or America, I thought my face was wrong. In Korea my eyes were too American; in America they were too Asian.

....

Living where I live today, in the eclectic society I love, it's hard to believe that my Amerasian face was so disconcerting. I was the town's only minority, and a pretty meager specimen I was. I can't imagine what people would have said to a black person or full-blooded Asian person. As it was, my face was ridiculed all the time. And at home I was never allowed to forget how different I looked. ("Elizabeth, don't pull your hair back like that. You look much more American when it's fluffed around your face. Don't stay out in the sun. You look like a red Indian or something, not a pretty little American girl.")

My adoptive mother was tall and slender, with light-brown hair that showed no signs of gray well into old age. She always dressed as if she were expecting company. On any day of the week you could come by the house at 7:00 A.M. and find her wearing stockings, a girdle, two-inch pumps, and a dress. She prided herself on never wearing makeup—other than rouge, lipstick, and powder. She got her hair permed once a month.

By this time Dad was pastor of a small fundamentalist church. He always wore a suit, even on Saturdays. Generally it was dark, with a white shirt and a dark tie. He was friendly to the outside world and genuinely interested in other people. His greatest charm was his ability to make everyone believe that seeing them had made his day, that their presence was all that was needed to make his happiness complete. And he was sincere.

He spent most of his time taking care of everyone else's needs. He visited the sick. He was at church whenever he was needed. He led services at local rest homes. He arranged for food vouchers when people had no money, and he took them to the store to get their groceries. But he was hardly ever home. Apart from my daily piano lessons and religious lectures, I was last on his list of priorities.

Dad was a study in contrasts. On one hand, his religion had left him with a very narrow view of right and wrong and the belief in absolute sin and absolute damnation. And yet he was an innately kind and loving man who could punish me harshly for a sinful thought and then spend the night on his knees, in tears, praying for my soul.

I desperately wanted to please him. And, for some reason, I felt responsible for his happiness. That feeling began after I'd been living with them just a couple of days. We were all in the kitchen and Mom handed me the last cookie from the cookie jar—a kind gesture that was out of character for her. I took it, then looked at Dad's face and immediately put the cookie in his mouth. He smiled and ate it, and I was overjoyed—I had done something to make him happy with me.

I continued to put cookies in his mouth over the years. Whenever we played a game—Monopoly sometimes, or

Aggravation—I cheated so that Dad would win. I cried whenever he appeared less than perfect or when he didn't get his way. At church camp one summer the kids sneaked his pajamas out of our cabin and hoisted them up on the flagpole, and I became hysterical and tried to lower the mechanism so no one could have a laugh at Dad's expense.

For some reason I became obsessed with protecting him. He seemed very vulnerable to me, despite the harshness with which he often treated me, and I thought it was my responsibility to keep him safe and happy.

Nevertheless, I made him angry a great deal of the time, and he continued to think my behavior was deliberate sinfulness. One December night about a year after my adoption, we had finished our evening Bible study, and it was my turn to pray. But as soon as I said "Dear Lord Jesus," I burst into tears. I had been feeling progressively more uneasy and desolate, without knowing why.

All of a sudden I knew.

"I feel like my mommy's dying," I told my shocked parents. "I feel like I'm going to die too. I want her back. Can't Jesus bring her back?" I was wracked with sobs and I couldn't articulate the depth of my anguish.

Dad was furious. "Stop crying immediately," he told me. "I mean it. Stop it this instant."

I tried my hardest, but I was too consumed by grief to shut it off, even though I knew he'd punish me—since my parents berated me for even having a sad look on my face, they viewed uncontrollable sobs as an outrage.

Dad slapped my face, back and forth, and the sobs diminished, turning into coughs, then gagging hiccups. The pain of forcing them down into my chest was excruciating. "She is not your mother!" he yelled at me. "She was a sinful woman who didn't love you at all. She's in hell. Do you think you know more than God? Are you criticizing His decisions? Do you know what happens to people who do that?"

And he proceeded to tell me, by reading me instance after instance in the Bible where someone had the temerity to second-guess God. In every case, the punishment was terrible. "God is a God of wrath!" Dad told me. "How dare you question His laws."

Mom sat quietly, watching the scene, shaking her head in disbelief at my sinfulness. "I'm just so, so sorry that you could be such a bad little girl," she told me. "I thought we had the Lord's own special child. He led us to choose you out of all the children in that orphanage, and I never thought you'd act this way."

I stood in front of them, my chest heaving painfully as I stared at the floor. I felt an increasingly familiar jumble of emotions: fear, anger, loneliness—but mostly shame.

Before too long, I learned to push Omma from my thoughts. My parents told me she was something very bad and sinful called a prostitute. She didn't love me, they said; it didn't matter to her whether I lived or died.

They had a stock phrase that was repeated ad nauseum throughout my growing-up years: "Your mother left you to die in a rice paddy." It was included in nearly every lecture or scolding or instruction: "Be more respectful to your mom. She loves you much more than your birth mother, who left you to die in a rice paddy." "Be obedient and do all your chores to the glory of God. Remember how lucky you are to be in America, since your birth mother left you to die in a rice paddy." "How can you displease God by crying over your birth mother? She didn't love you at all. Remember, she didn't want you. She left you to die in a rice paddy."

A few years ago I pinned my parents down about that phrase.

Why had they said it? What made them think it? Mom said she was sure someone had told them that at some point. Dad, however, admitted that they just made it up. He said they thought it would be easier for me to believe that story. Easier than what, he didn't say. We never went any further into the issue. I said it was okay, that I was sure they acted for the best. I still didn't want to upset them.

....

My parents said that Omma didn't accept Jesus as her Savior, and so now she's in hell, where she'll burn for all eternity. I was tormented constantly with thoughts of death and hell and eternal damnation. I always found it ironic that in fundamentalist Christianity, the thought of the afterlife is touted as something comforting, and yet the whole concept is so terrifying. My parents said we were always surrounded by legions of demons who were waiting to clutch our souls and carry us off to hell. In my mind, the demons were very real. I saw them in my imagination, bending over me, waiting. They were tall, scaly creatures with huge hands that ended in jagged claws. They had gaping mouths with razor-sharp teeth. As nighttime approached, they seemed more menacing. While I brushed my teeth and washed my face and put on my pajamas, my fear grew.

The only protection was prayer. I knelt on the threadbare rug in my bedroom reciting my litany of sins from the day: "I had an angry thought today. I talked back to Dad today. I felt envy today." I cleansed my soul for fifteen or twenty minutes because one unconfessed sin meant the demons could get me. My eyes were closed, but every few seconds I cracked one eyelid a tiny bit to peep out. My parents said that angels and demons could be seen only with spiritual eyes, not with physical ones. And they said that during prayer, our spiritual eyes were opened. So I was on the watch for demons during prayer time.

After praying I climbed into bed and turned out the light. I tried to trick the demons I knew were hiding from me by pretending to be asleep and then opening my eyes very quickly, scanning the corners of the room. Sometimes I almost saw them. Sometimes I thought the demons in the Bosch triptych moved around, and maybe they were the ones lurking in the dark.

Hell was as real to me as the nightmares that besieged me every night. Both had more reality than my waking life. I didn't feel real at all. When I looked in the mirror I was sometimes caught by surprise to see a face looking back at me. I thought I was probably someone's bad dream, and I felt sorry for them. But eventually, I assumed, the dreamer would awaken into a sunlit world and I would vanish like the last dark tendril of candle smoke.

In the pink brick house I lay curled in my Early American bed wearing my flannel nightie. I read the Bible and said my prayer, and as the image inched closer I drew my knees up tight and whispered "Jesus, Jesus" over and over. But He never came.

There, see it gathering? In the corner of my room, forming itself into a woman's body, suspended between heaven and earth. I can't see her face, but her bare feet are elongated and limp, the toes pointing straight down to my braided rag rug, which has somehow become a neatly swept earth floor. She's wearing a white dress, trimmed in blue and crossed with a sash at the bodice. Now she's starting to move slightly in the breeze from my open window. I have to open my eyes before her face turns toward me. Jesus. Jesus. I push myself up to the ceiling. If I can touch the ceiling I'll wake up. Jesus. Omma.

In the darkest hour of night I lay panting in bed, my heart

pounding so loud it hurt my ears, my head drenched in sweat, and my fingernails clogged with my skin and blood.

....

I was told over and over how blessed I was to have been adopted by my parents and taken into a Christian family, out of Korea and the orphanage. "All those other children died, and God chose you to live," my parents told me. "Of all the orphans there, He led us to adopt you. God has a very special plan for your life, and you must always obey and honor Him." I trembled when I thought of how I was letting God down every minute. He should have chosen someone else.

I had terrible feelings of guilt about those other children. My parents shook their heads and looked solemn as they recounted the atrocities committed against the forgotten children of the Korean War. I thought about the ones I had known personally—the little girl in the trash can, the little boy without hands—and I couldn't imagine why I was worth saving and they weren't.

My parents reminded me daily of all the children sleeping in back alleys in Seoul and scrambling for a few bites of food, and they contrasted that world with the comfortable home I'd been given. I was haunted by the suffering of those children. I was angry over the injustice that left them there and brought me to America. I prayed for them—because I didn't know what else to do—but it felt like wasted effort. I was angry with God for the choice He made: I wasn't worth saving, and maybe they were.

I wondered if there was a quota of children who could be rescued, and after it was filled all the rest were tossed out like so much cosmic garbage. I was also afraid of having thoughts like that; I was afraid of God's wrath and retribution.

During family Bible time we talked about the doctrine of

"predestination." Dad explained it by saying predestination means that God chose certain people—the Bible says "even before the foundation of the world"—to be saved. A few people got lucky; the rest will spend eternity in hell. It sounded like the work of a sadistic lunatic to me, but my parents explained that because we think with earthly minds, we aren't wise enough to understand why God does what He does. In the Book of Isaiah God says "For My thoughts are not your thoughts, neither are your ways My ways."

And to start screaming and beating my fists against my face because God didn't choose my Omma to be saved was just plain sinful, my parents said. If she's in hell it's because of her own evil nature, and what I better do is accept the will of God.

Fear ruled my life. I was afraid of my parents. I was afraid of God and of hell. I was afraid of the kids at school who whispered about me and giggled. I was afraid I'd get sent back to the orphanage. I was afraid of going to sleep. I was afraid of the glow-in-the-dark head of Christ wearing the crown of thorns hanging in the hallway.

....

My parents tape-recorded many hours of my childhood on a big reel-to-reel machine that sat in the corner of the living room. Many of the vignettes were of punishment. The story would unfold—usually centered around my fear of something—and would progress through the reasoning, the pleading, the tears, and the denouement of my punishment and contrition.

The tape recorder was always at the ready. When a crisis happened—for example, I hadn't memorized a Bible verse properly, or I was afraid to go down in the basement—Dad would get up and turn on the tape recorder. He'd pace back and forth, preaching at me while I tried not to cry. I was always aware that the tape recorder was running, but it was so routine that I didn't think it was anything odd.

Quite often he'd spank me while the machine was recording. Listening to the tapes later, every slap would come through clearly, along with my sobs. In the background Mom could be heard saying something like "Now, aren't you sorry you were such a bad little girl? Don't you want to ask Jesus to forgive you?"

The tape recordings went on until I was about ten. They got played over and over as I was growing up, and we sat in the living room and listened. My parents loved them. The tape recordings formed the nucleus of our family entertainment. We sat in the living room after dinner, and Mom would say "Oh, let's hear one of those cute tapes of Elizabeth."

During the scenes where I was screaming or begging, my parents would chuckle and shake their heads at me. It was all supposed to be amusing and also an object lesson in the wages of sin. I tried to smile along with them, and as I got older I learned to laugh aloud at my tape-recorded misery.

I also began commenting on the despicable child in those tapes. "Listen to me," I'd tell my parents. "I was really bad, wasn't I? How could you put up with me? I really deserved a spanking for that one."

A few years ago Dad had all the reel-to-reels transferred to cassettes and gave me a leather-bound portfolio with copies of all the tapes as a Christmas present. Stunned, I thanked him and then shoved them in the back of a drawer. I never listened to them and never took them out of the drawer until a couple of years ago, when I gathered them up in a cathartic flurry of housecleaning and threw them away.

This is one of the abnormalities of my parents' household that I simply accepted as the norm. It surprises me how incredulous people are about it, even though now I realize how bizarre it was. But the tape recordings were, for me, as routine a part of everyday life as washing the breakfast dishes. People acting out of over-the-top religious fanaticism do things that are incomprehensible to others. The tape recordings were just part and parcel of that punitive, harshly fundamentalist household.

Chapter Eight

My little circle of Mom, Dad, and church was suddenly and uncomfortably expanded when I was enrolled in school. I had learned enough of the rules at home and church to get by, but school was yet another strange and uncongenial world.

On my first day at school, my teacher introduced me to the class, then told me to say something about myself. I stood there, silent, fidgeting with the satin sash on my too dressy dress. I didn't know what to say. My parents didn't like me to talk about Korea, so I couldn't tell the kids where I was from. I didn't have any friends or hobbies to talk about. I had no pets to describe. There was nothing I could think of that anyone would be even remotely interested in. I bowed slightly when the teacher introduced me, and the kids snickered. The teacher waited for a few seconds, then brusquely told me to sit down.

By this time I'd been in America a little more than a year, and I was presumed to be about seven. I had already gone through the American naturalization process, and my knowledge of American history and the fine points of the English language was more comprehensive than most of my classmates. On that first day I drew a picture in my notebook while the teacher talked. She asked if she was boring me and I answered truthfully: "Yes." So I spent the next hour in the corner, not quite sure how I got there or what I was supposed to do.

My adoptive parents taught me how to read before I started school, and they did such a good job that my second-grade teacher amended her opinion of me after a few days and decided I was a prodigy. I had to read aloud to the sixth-grade students out of their English textbook. The teacher told them they should be ashamed that a second-grader who had known English for only a short time could read so much better than they did.

That, of course, sealed my fate at school. The students, especially the older ones, were merciless. They made fun of my curly, tempestuous hair. They made fun of my mildly slanted eyes and blunt nose. They made fun of the precise way I articulated my words and my occasional Korean accent. And since everyone in our tiny town knew my parents, the kids also knew I was adopted, so they naturally made fun of that.

Throughout elementary school things were pretty much the same: I was smart but I was miserable. I had no friends and I was the constant butt of the playground jokes. I ate lunch alone; I sat at the far end of the playground during recess, reading Charles Dickens.

I loved Dickens. When I read him I felt as if he were talking just to me, and that he understood exactly how sad and lonely I felt. I was searching for an emotional road map that I could follow to help get me through the years of alienation. No one in real life had taught me how to deal with loss and abandonment, but I discovered that literature could connect me with something larger than my own life, and I was transported.

In fifth grade I did a book report on *David Copperfield*. I decided this would be the best book report in history and my classmates would finally accept me because the story of David Copperfield's misery would move them to open their hearts. I made two family trees: one to show David's biological family and another one to show his true, emotional family. I told about how unloved and neglected he was. I recited the final, embarrassingly ornate passage about Agnes "pointing upward."

In front of me the students fidgeted and whispered. I saw kids yawning, giving each other half-smiles, doodling in their notebooks.

When I finished and sat down at my desk the boy behind me leaned forward and said, "That was the stupidest book report ever, weirdo."

The one instance in which I had some measure of camaraderie with other kids during that period was when one of my few short-lived pets—a rescued greyhound given me by a church member—watched me get on the bus and then chased it twelve miles from our house to the school.

The other kids on the school bus first called my attention to the chase. "Look at your dog. He's chasing the bus. He doesn't want you to leave." I felt a welling up of love for the dog; of awe and gratitude that another creature thought enough of me to run on hot asphalt and sandy desert back roads just to be near me. My chest got tight and my throat burned as I watched him through the bus's wide rear window.

As he loped steadily along behind the bus, his tongue hanging out and his slender legs sending up clouds of dirt, the kids on the bus cheered him on. "All right! Good boy! Wow, your dog is really cool." I felt almost accepted by the kids in those moments. Because they admired my dog—and my dog obviously loved me—they were actually speaking to me. We were united in watching my cool dog chase the bus.

Once we got to school I gave him some water while the kids gathered around, patted his head and stroked his sleek flanks, and asked me questions about him. He wagged politely at them but saved his licks and nuzzles for me. I called my parents to come to school and pick him up.

They did, but that afternoon when I got home from school the dog was gone. "We can't be running all over creation picking up that dog," they said. "He was supposed to stay put. He's too much trouble."

I found out that my parents took that beautiful dog to the pound, and I agonized over his fate—discarded again, locked in a cage, probably dying unwanted and afraid. I promised myself that one day I would give a child of mine a pet that would never get taken away.

....

My parents were the teachers; their home was the classroom. Every moment of every day the lessons were hammered home: The Bible is the literal word of God; Christ is the only atonement for sins; fear or grief or anger or curiosity or desire is of Satan; obedience must be immediate, unquestioning, and absolute.

It frustrated them that I was so afraid of so many things. During interminable sessions in the living room after the evening family "devotions," or Bible and prayer time, they explained to me why my fear was so sinful. They had me memorize Matthew 10:28: "And do not fear those who kill the body, but are unable to kill the soul; but rather fear Him who is able to destroy both soul and body in hell."

And what if God did decide He was going to end my life? The Bible has an answer to that as well: "Though He slay me, yet will I trust Him."

I was acutely aware of my many flaws. In Korea I was sub-human. Now I was sub-Christlike. I knew I wasn't good enough for anyone, and I felt complete despair. I couldn't measure up to anyone's standards. My parents told me I was saved from Korea to be re-created into God's image, but I wasn't a malleable enough piece of clay.

As repetitive as all this sounds, it's impossible to do justice to the stultifying monotony of my life in that household. I was trapped on a wheel that turned endlessly on the same theme.

....

More and more, books were my salvation. I began devouring whatever was available on the shelves in our house. Dad's office was lined with books, floor-to-ceiling shelves holding collected sermons and theological treatises and about two dozen Bibles—family Bibles, heirloom Bibles, gift Bibles, New American Standard, King James, Hebrew, and Greek. But there were a few gems scattered in there as well: Shakespeare and Austen and Dickens, to name a few. Reading became the way I escaped the gray confines of life in this fundamentalist Christian home in a tiny town in a lonely, vast desert.

When I was about ten, I went with my parents to visit a woman in our church. I hated those visits to "shut-ins," where I had to sit perfectly still and smile and listen to banal adult conversation and pretend to be interested. But this time something amazing happened.

The woman we visited lived in a trailer, every surface littered with knickknacks: china kittens with plaid bows around their necks and decorative plates on stands. In the jumble was a slender book of poems with stiff covers, and pages that looked as if they'd never been opened. I asked if I could read it, and the woman said I could as long as I didn't get it dirty or tear it. I took the book to her kitchen table and laid it carefully on a plastic place mat that was shaped like a butterfly.

That afternoon changed my life. Sitting in that cluttered room, with the motes of dust dancing in the sunlight, I found out I wasn't alone.

The poem I read was written by someone who had just lost a dearly loved companion, and it haunted me for years. "What is my life to me? And what am I to life?/A ship whose star has guttered out. A fear that in the deep night starts awake" . . . were the only two lines I could remember. I didn't know who the author was. It got to the point where I almost believed I dreamed up the lines myself.

When I entered my teens I started searching for that poem, for that author. But in our little town library there were only a few books of poetry, and none of them was what I wanted. Nevertheless, I kept looking.

After my first encounter with poetry, I began trying to write it myself. It was pretty bad, but my teachers liked it and it usually got thumbtacked to the bulletin board at my elementary school. I tried haiku and limericks, and wrote about the topics that teachers gave A grades for, rain and sunsets and peace on earth. The real poetry of raw emotions was private, and no one but me read the things I wrote in my diary:

You say that I'm ugly
You say that I'm strange.
I've swallowed every word
Each searing drop of pain.
Life has shoved the facts
down my constricted throat
Life, you can force-feed me
on anguish till I choke.
So I cry cause life's unfair?
Sorry, bitch, that's tough.
I am not worth the joys of earth
I am not meant for love.

God is Good, they say.
I'm not so sure.
I think God may be a mad scientist
in a white lab coat
experimenting on cages of people.
Maybe He laughs when we run around
screaming and screaming.
Maybe He takes notes on us under little headings:
"control group"
"test group"
as He watches us weep silently in corners
gnawing on our fingers.
Or maybe He's asleep in His bedroom upstairs
underneath His silken canopy,

while we howl in anguish down in the basement
rotting in our rusty cages
completely forgotten by God the Mad Scientist.

We have no idea of another's suffering.
I judge you, you judge me; we look askance
at hair or clothes or skin or smiles or the lack of smiles.
I think you laugh too loudly and I hate your taste in music.
You think I talk too much and you hate the boots I wear.
And all the while inside we weep and weep and weep.
We peek out, terrified, on a world that doesn't know us,
and long for someone to see how lovable we are.
We pass each other by, faces careful masks of unconcern.
Your anguish cries to mine; my heart aches just like yours.

My parents found my diary once, when I was in sixth grade, and there was hell to pay. It was the kind that had a little lock on its clasp, and I naïvely assumed it would open only with the key I kept under my mattress.

But the lock opened with just a little twiddling of the dial, and when I got home from school I found my parents waiting, stony-faced. Dad had opened the diary, and not only had they read it, but they had also made an appointment with my school principal to share with him what they'd found and make sure I was punished for the things I wrote about my teachers and classmates.

I wrote about practicing "French kissing" on my pillow so I'd be good at it someday. I wrote about my sixth-grade teacher, who was cool because she said "dammit." I wrote about a girl who called me an "ugly Chink" and how I hoped she went to hell and burned for all eternity.

After what seemed like hours of listening to my parents rant and rave about my evil nature, I was sent to my room to read the Bible. I wasn't spanked for what had happened, but a much worse punishment was devised. The next day my parents and I trooped into the school principal's office, where I had to read him what I'd written. We sat in front of his desk and I read the entries, my voice and hands shaking. Several times he tried to interrupt, but my parents said I wasn't quite finished. I think he was nonplussed by the whole thing—he seemed somewhat sympathetic to me and a bit brusque with my parents. Nevertheless, at my parents' urging, I got detention for a week.

My parents didn't comment on the poetry I had written in my diary, even though it had "bad language" and blasphemous references to God. I don't think they read it, since it was in verse. Poetry didn't interest them at all—I don't know if they even recognized it.

For me there was a real, earthy comfort to be found in poetry, whether it was my own fumbling verses or exquisite Shakespearean sonnets such as: "Farewell! thou art too dear for my possessing." I learned that the theme of loss was universal, and that made me feel less alone. I learned that any pain in my life had been felt by countless others in countless past lifetimes and would be felt by people in lifetimes yet to come.

Poetry first introduced me to the concept that pain could, perhaps, be viewed as "the pain" and not "my pain." That sorrow and loneliness and abandonment were the human condition, not my sole possession.

Meanwhile, I kept trying to fit in. I watched the way Americans moved, talked, used their hands; and I became a master at imitation. I had a better understanding of the language than the American-born children I went to school with. So why couldn't my face change too? Why couldn't those Asian eyes become round and blue? Why didn't my despised hair lighten to blond? Why couldn't my blunt, abbreviated nose develop a more angular line?

At school events, I stood on stage—either singing or reciting something or getting an award—and looked out at the small, smug gathering of homogeneous Anglo children, hating every one of them. Always, looking back at me, were a few with their fingers held at the corners of their eyes, pulling up and out, mocking the outcast before them.

....

Hidden in the back of my bedroom closet, behind the box of quilt-square scraps I hemmed each week for the Women's Missionary Society at church, was my secret.

I had fashioned a blond wig by cutting strips of paper carefully, all the same width and length, and coloring them on both sides with the yellow crayon from my box. They were sewn together at one end, and I draped the blond fall over my head when I was alone in my room.

Then I became an American-born girl, and my face was my birthright to acceptance. My name was Cindy. I was on the cheerleading squad. I had some freckles across my nose, and my eyes were as blue as forget-me-nots. I was tall and slender, and on my bedroom walls were my cheerleading pom-poms, a school pennant, and pictures of cute boys cut from magazines. There was a pink Princess-style telephone on my bedside table, along with a vinyl-covered address and phone book that was full of numbers—I was the most popular girl in school. My closet was chaotic, stuffed with culottes and miniskirts and matching outfits and shoes.

In reality, my bedroom walls had nothing but religious pictures on them. The bedside table held a Bible and a lamp. No magazines were allowed, even if I had somehow found money to buy them. I made my own dresses out of fabric from a discount store where Mom shopped, and I wore them over and over. Because of the rules about Christian clothing laid down by my parents, the dresses were dowdy and plain. It was the late 1960s, and fashion dictated miniskirts, knee-high boots, hip-hugger jeans, and halter tops. My dresses hit at mid-calf. They had puffy sleeves and round collars.

At school, those dresses were good for lots of laughs.

I had learned to sew at church, at the Saturday afternoon Women's Missionary Society meetings. We made quilts, baby clothes, and basic things like A-line skirts to be sent off to missionaries. Under the tutelage of the church women I learned how to make darts, install flat zippers, whipstitch buttonholes, and put in facings. By seventh grade I made all my own clothes, except for underwear.

I told my parents that the kids at school made fun of me and how ostracized I was. I thought one reason was the way I dressed, so I asked if I could baby-sit for someone in the church and earn extra money for clothes. I wanted culottes and blue jeans and sweatshirts like everyone else wore, instead of floral-patterned dresses made out of no-iron polyester. Dad thought the request was ridiculous and treated it crisply. "Why are you so concerned with worldly desires? 'For man looketh on the outward appearance, but God looketh on the heart.' You make sure your heart is pure. What others think of you doesn't matter. 'God draws near to the humble, but the proud He knoweth afar off.' And besides, your work is here in your home and at the church. You don't have time to work in other people's homes."

My parents decided that since I obviously had an unholy obsession with clothes, a lesson in humility was needed. At dinner that night, Mom laid down the new rule.

"Your father and I have been praying about how to break you of your worldly attitude about clothing. From now on you can wear one dress a week. You can rotate the dress from week to week, but you'll wear the same one Monday through Friday. On Sundays you can wear your good dress."

I was horrified. It hadn't occurred to me that they might suggest such a thing. I realized I'd made a huge tactical mistake, and I began backpedaling in panic.

"Please don't make me do that. I won't have a worldly attitude anymore about clothes, I promise. I won't ask for anything more. Please, please, please. The kids will make so much fun of me. I'll die if you make me do this."

"See? This is exactly what we mean about your worldly attitude. You should be happy that you have a nice dress to wear at all. Children in Korea don't even have a nice dress like you have. They'd be so grateful for it. We brought you out of the orphanage and gave you everything you need, and still you want more. If other kids make fun of you, you should consider it a blessing. You're being crucified with Christ so that you can share in his eternal glory."

I had skipped two grades, so I was already a couple of years younger than most of my classmates, and they seemed light-years ahead of me in sophistication. I knew I'd never fit in with them. And after a while, the kids didn't make fun of my dress anymore. They just ignored me.

So from then through junior high school, I wore the same dress five days a week. Once I got to high school, my parents relented and I was allowed to make five outfits, one for each day of the school week. They were still dowdy dresses, but at least there were five of them.

As I got older, I became increasingly afraid of God and of His list of demands. The Bible says, "Be ye perfect, even as your Father in heaven is perfect." This seemed impossible. I had to ask forgiveness all the time, since even our thoughts are judged. It was a no-win situation. If I got angry but I managed to bite back the words, I still had to ask forgiveness for the angry thought. And if I felt proud of myself for not speaking angrily, I had to ask forgiveness for pride. If I had a sexual thought, I had to ask forgiveness for that. But asking forgiveness reminded me of the thought, so I couldn't purge it completely from my mind. It was an unending circle with no way out.

My biggest fear was that I'd die unexpectedly before I had a chance to ask forgiveness for the latest sinful thought, and I'd go to hell.

In our church the subject of hell got lots of attention. In hell, I was told, there is wailing and gnashing of teeth, and the damned are cast into the lake of fire, which burns hotter than anything imaginable, for all eternity. The people there can see what it's like in heaven, so their anguish is intensified by looking upon unattainable bliss. I could understand that feeling; I'd looked upon unattainable bliss most of my life.

My parents said everyone in hell knew they could have been in heaven with Jesus, if only they'd accepted Him. But if they had never heard about Him in the first place, that seemed outrageously unfair to me, no matter what my parents said about predestination.

Sometimes I wondered if God was just laughing away somewhere as we frantically tried to follow His impossible rules. I tried to squelch that thought, though, because my fear of God's judgment overpowered everything, even rational thought.

When I felt rebellious, I tried to debate the issue logically with my parents: I told them I thought predestination was just another word for prejudice; obviously the same God who made the Korean rule that children with mixed blood are less than human made the American rule that only born-again Christians can go to heaven. They told me I was guilty of blasphemy.

It was getting so that I was guilty of something nearly all the time—sins of commission or omission—but I still looked for ways to please my unpleasant parents. One way I knew I could placate them was to study the piano. They had big goals for me musically—I think they wanted me to be a wandering musical missionary, spreading the gospel of Christ and the culture of classical music all at the same time.

I was still taking daily piano lessons from Dad, and began playing in church by the time I was ten. Nevertheless, the piano was a constant source of anxiety for me, whether I was practicing at home in front of my parents or performing in public. I didn't mind playing the hymns at church, because any reasonably competent pianist can do that, but I hated recitals.

Dad volunteered me quite often for recitals, either at the church or at the community center. When I was twelve I played Beethoven's Pathétique—all three of the sonata's movements from memory—and shook uncontrollably the entire time. My execution was adequate until the third movement, when I missed the fingering on an arpeggio. Out of the corner of my eye I saw Dad shake his head and switch his gaze from me to the floor, and my heart sank. When the recital ended he wouldn't speak to me, and the familiar wave of loneliness and nausea swept over me.

....

Before I knew it, I was the household's full-time housekeeper and cook. I was living a life of more civilized slavery than the one Omma had protected me from, but all the daily chores— from scrubbing the toilets to cooking each meal—were mine.

The contrast between the two mothers in my life was great: Omma worked so hard day after day and still kept things tidy and found time to pamper her child. Mom did pretty much nothing except lie on the sofa and dress up for church functions.

I was aware that other kids didn't have the same chores I had—I heard kids talk at school about what their moms made for dinner the previous night, for example—and I was consumed with jealousy.

Of course, since jealousy was a sin, I was also consumed with guilt.

Chapter Nine

Just when I thought I had the rhythms of the house figured out and under control, Mom's mother came to live with us. I was in fifth grade and believed she embodied the worst characteristics of my parents. Everything about them that gave me pain was magnified in her. And in her view, it was obvious that adopting me was the biggest mistake my parents ever made. One day after a sex education class in school I was filled with childish curiosity and asked Mom if she and Dad had intercourse. Grandmother turned to Mom in triumph. "See? She's completely degenerate. That's what you get."

Grandmother didn't want them to adopt a Korean child. She thought that anyone nonwhite was barbaric, and she was very proud of the blond hair and blue eyes that ran in her family. She referred to my eyes as "mud-colored." Her insular arrogance affected everything she did. Before she moved in with us she had a house nearby, where she employed a black gardener. He was not allowed in the house, although she conceded that he was "a good worker." On Friday afternoons, before he went home, she handed him a bottle of 7-Up, and he drank it on the back porch. He got the bottle because Grandmother said she didn't want a colored dirtying up her good cut-glass tumblers.

I decided I wanted to be just like him: He had a wry wit and the same respect for growing things that Omma had.

To me he was a nice, funny person who treated me like an equal. To my grandmother he was there simply for her use. He never said anything when Grandmother handed him his 7-Up bottle, but he looked deadpan at me and raised one eyebrow, and I burst out laughing. We would talk about how funny people are, and about flowers.

I decided I wanted to drink my 7-Up out of a bottle too and wear overalls and learn how to prune roses. Grandmother was horrified and told my parents, who explained that certain proprieties must be maintained in a nice society.

Although I didn't understand what those proprieties were, I began to see that even in America I was not the only one isolated and hated simply because I didn't look the same as people around me.

....

Grandmother was a short, sturdy woman. She was less than five feet tall, and wore support hose and lace-up orthopedic shoes.

She had her hair done every week at the one beauty parlor in town, and she wore a freshly ironed dress every day. She didn't like colored folks, Orientals, Jews, or hippies. She often said the world was headed toward destruction.

She smiled only at church, where she had a special seat in the second pew from the front. Her sacred cushion stayed on that seat, and woe to any hapless stranger who sat there by mistake.

After she had a mild stroke, Grandmother decided to move in with us. Her husband, whom I never met, had already been dead for many years. She ruled the house with her withered iron fist, and both my parents obeyed her. I learned later that she had loaned them the money to buy their house, with the proviso that she would live there with them. The one television set in the house was in her room, as was an upholstered armchair and ottoman.

With Grandmother's arrival my already massive list of daily chores expanded to include all of her needs. Though there was nothing to stop her from taking care of herself, she viewed everyone around her—especially those who weren't of pure Aryan stock—as her servants.

I had to help her bathe and dress and clean her dentures. Being that close to her made me gag. I hated her musty smell and her clacking teeth and her supercilious ways. She walked with a cane, and if I didn't do what she wanted quickly enough or if I was in her way she whacked me across the legs with it. She berated me constantly. She said I was slow, rebellious, clumsy.

Grandmother often told me that people should "stick to their own kind," and that mixing the races never worked. She said it was too bad that I'd never be as pretty as an American child. Once after she said that I got up in the night and went into the bathroom I shared with her and moved her dentures from the fizzy glass of Polident by the sink to the top row of the medicine chest. After a long, frantic search the next day, Mom found them.

"Well, Grandmother," I said, "sometimes when people get old they start to lose their minds and they begin putting things in strange places. I guess that's what happening to you. It's too bad that you'll never be young and smart again."

Grandmother's bedroom was next to mine, and we shared the bathroom that was connected to her room. Her room was large and sunny, but she kept the curtains closed because she had cataracts on her eyes and the light bothered her. She sat in the easy chair throughout the day, watching *As the World Turns* and *General Hospital*. From time to time she hollered at me to bring her something: a glass of water, a hankie, or the *TV Guide* and her magnifying glass.

My room had one window, but I was supposed to keep the curtain closed because the sunlight would fade the furniture. Since the furniture was a walnut four-poster bed and a dresser from Sears, I didn't quite understand such concern. Nevertheless, I did what I was told.

Our shared bathroom had been built as a master bathroom, and it had two sinks side by side. Grandmother's medicines, her denture glass, her eye drops, and her Epsom salts took up most of the counter space. I hated using the same toilet she used or drying my hands on the same towel.

Around this time I began to indulge myself with small acts of rebellion. My attitude toward my family was slowly changing—no longer was I completely focused on pleasing them. Instead I was starting to look at ways to please myself. I was also starting to feel a healthy contempt for much of what I had once simply accepted. And I was beginning to develop a sense of humor, even though I was the only one laughing at my jokes. I sometimes played pranks on Grandmother that made me laugh hysterically but also got me into trouble.

For example, Grandmother was extremely possessive about the

easy chair in front of her television set. No one else was allowed to sit there, because she said the cushions were arranged "just so" and she didn't want them disturbed. I had a doll that was almost as tall as I was. It had been a Christmas present and was supposed to walk alongside you if you held its hand. The walking mechanism never worked, and the doll was too big and unwieldy to play with, so it usually was shoved in the back of my closet.

One day, while Grandmother was in the bathroom, I put the doll in her easy chair. I put a fuzzy black hat of Mom's on the doll's head. I turned the chair so just part of the doll was visible from the bedroom doorway. With Grandmother's cataracts, I figured, she'd mistake the doll for me and think I was sitting in her chair. I hid in her closet and waited.

I heard the bathroom door open and Grandmother's cane thudding on the floor. She opened her bedroom door and stopped, and I watched her from the four-inch opening in the closet door. "Elizabeth! You get out of my chair this instant, young lady! You know perfectly good and well you're not allowed there. Now you've ruined the cushions. Do you hear me? I said get out. I have never seen such an evil child. You're going to get punishment like you've never had before, Miss Disobedient."

Grandmother was enraged. Her dentures slipped and clacked as she yelled at the doll. I clamped my hand over my mouth so I wouldn't laugh out loud. She hobbled forward and lifted her cane, then whacked the doll across the arm, scolding all the while. The doll teetered for a couple of seconds, then tilted. The black fuzzy hat fell to the floor and the doll toppled over onto its head. Grandmother screamed and dropped her cane. I fell out of the closet, laughing.

My parents came running in, and when they figured out what happened I got what Grandmother called "a thrashing to drive out Satan." But even though I was sore for a couple of days, the joke was worth it.

Since Grandmother's world revolved around her television set, most of my practical jokes did as well. I did small, spiteful things: I sneaked into her room whenever she got up to go to the bathroom—as she did quite often—and changed the channel. So when she got back she'd mutter to herself, then heave herself back up and hobble to the television to change it back. "What in the world? This crazy TV keeps going away from the right channel. I'm going to call a repairman one of these days."

At church Grandmother was gracious and sweet, in a somewhat acidulated way, and people commented to me about her. "Oh, your grandma is just the cutest thing! She sits in her special place like a little queen. I bet you just love your grandma, don't you?" I usually didn't even bother to nod—I'd just look incredulously at whoever was speaking. How could anyone love that withered, malevolent old hag?

....

In Mom's interaction with Grandmother, I saw the same drama of dominance and shame played out a generation once removed. Years later I recalled the degrading and insulting way Grandmother spoke to Mom and realized that so much of what Mom did to me was an echo of her own childhood. It was when my own daughter was born that I had to confront what I knew of being a mother. Although Omma gave me love and acceptance, she also left me after too short a time. It was that brief period of pure love that served as my model for motherhood. But it was incomplete. There were only fragments of warmth to cling to, and the rest of the process had to be learned.

Once a week Grandmother got a full bath. On Saturday evenings she went in the bathroom and took off all her clothes, leaving them in a pile on the floor for me to pick up. Then I held her arm while she stepped into the tub and sat on a plastic stool. I used a pitcher to rinse her off and then lathered up her washcloth with the bar of Palmolive soap. I washed her, starting at her neck and working down. She lifted her arms so I could wash her armpits and stood up slightly, leaning heavily on my shoulders, so I could wash her buttocks. Her smell was nauseating. I held my breath and averted my eyes, and turned my head away every few seconds to gulp lungsful of air.

She talked to me throughout the bath: "Make sure you scrub my back thoroughly. You missed a spot last time. Stand still while I lean on you. You're going to make me fall if you're not careful. My bottom's sore. Make sure you rinse it carefully. Don't be so clumsy."

After her bath, she leaned on me again as she stepped out. Every time she leaned on me, whether at bathtime or when she was getting in and out of the car, she dug her fingernails into the hollows around my shoulders and collarbones. Grandmother was a bony woman whose leathery skin hung in pouches from her body. She was a small woman, but when she leaned on me it felt like she weighed a ton.

In the bathroom I dried her off, trying to keep a couple of layers of toweling between my hand and her body. I tried my best not to touch her withered skin, and sometimes the revulsion I felt would show in my face and she'd snap at me. "What's the matter with you? You look like you swallowed a lemon."

She put on her nightgown and clean underwear and stood at the bathroom sink, cleaning her dentures. I picked up her dirty clothes by their edges and put them in the bathroom hamper, only to have to touch them again when I did the laundry.

....

I had mixed feelings about bodies. I felt revulsion toward Grandmother's naked body, which I was forced to see on a regular basis. I was ashamed of my own body and budding womanhood. I knew my body was supposed to be the temple of God, so I felt no ownership over it. During communion we ate the body and blood of the Lord, which added another layer to my stack of body issues.

My first experience with discovering my body and what it could do and how it could feel ended grotesquely. I was about ten. At that age I knew nothing about sex. My parents, of course, disapproved of anything that involved physical pleasure. Sex was discussed only in the context of the evils of fornication and adultery and the horrible fate that awaited anyone who did those things. I was in bed one morning, just awakened, and drowsily started touching myself. I didn't know enough about sex to know that it might be wrong. I had never heard the word "masturbation." I had never heard the word "clitoris." All I knew was that it was a new sensation and I wanted to explore it further. Mom came in to get me out of bed and saw what I was doing. She was horrified and I realized immediately, of course, that I had done something terrible, but I didn't yet know just how terrible it was. She and Grandmother took me into the bathroom and made me take off my clothes and get into the tub.

The entire time they both berated me, saying I was filthy and disgusting. Mom kept saying, "Aren't you ashamed of yourself? How could you do something like that? I thought you were a good Christian girl." Mom held me down in the tub, with my legs pulled apart so I couldn't clamp my knees together, and Grandmother turned on the hot water tap full force.

The water was scalding and terribly painful. After a few minutes they let me up, and I promised fervently never to do anything so evil again.

Another incident took place around that same age. I'd taken my evening bath and put on talcum powder. I was clean and wearing warm flannel pajamas. I reveled in the sensuality of being clean and soft with the cotton flannel next to my skin, my hair damp and curly from the steam in the bathroom. I got into bed and my parents came in to hear me say my prayer. After I did that, as I was saying good night, I blurted out what I was feeling at the moment.

"I love feeling like this. I love being clean and warm. I like the way I smell. I wish I was married so my husband could enjoy me too." I remember feeling gratitude for the ability to feel that way, to really enjoy my skin and hair and scent and softness. I knew that marriage was a "holy estate, ordained of God," that it was okay to want to be married. In fact, my parents said a godly young woman's goal was to be married. So it seemed to me that I was thanking God for that in my future.

Dad, however, was immediately censorious and indignant. Was I feeling lustful? Was I harboring evil desires?

I didn't even know what lustful feelings were, but I felt guilty and confused. I was bewildered that something that felt so pure and sweet could make my parents so angry. I said, "No, Daddy, I'm not feeling lustful. I just wish I was married." Dad launched into a extemporaneous sermon: Why would I wish I was married when I was still a little girl? And why would I even think of things like that? And why was I focused on my body? I shouldn't even give that a second thought. I shouldn't be so attached to pleasures of the flesh.

So I knew, once again, I had said the wrong thing, done the wrong thing, and not only that, but felt the wrong thing. Even my very feelings were wrong.

Growing up in that household, my feelings came in for daily scrutiny. Because, as Dad pointed out, it was what was in our hearts that counted. God knew our hearts and thoughts, and we'd be judged accordingly. It wasn't enough to do the right thing or keep yourself completely sinless in your actions and words. Your thoughts were judged as well; therefore there was no escaping sin. So even to feel that moment of bliss because of the warmth and the smell and softness of my skin was wrong.

After a long, angry tirade, Dad made me get out of bed and get on my knees and ask God to forgive me for my lustful thoughts and for my preoccupation with the physical world.

....

Today, I would rather be intimate with someone than do just about anything. It isn't just the bliss of sex. It's physical closeness that I love; the sensuality and comfort and gloriousness of body touching body is something I never get enough of. And even as a child I found it incomprehensible when my parents would talk about the evils of the flesh and of desire. Both of them told me quite often as I was growing up that sex was not something they had any interest in, and it was something I shouldn't have any interest in.

What amazes me is that as an adult, I'm enthralled by sex. I love everything about it; I'm extremely aware of the physical world and its attendant pleasures and pains, and I'm acutely grateful for every nuance of physical feeling.

....

Grandmother had a couple more strokes as the years went by, and her health deteriorated. Finally she was bedridden, able only to nod or shake her head. The day she died was the one and only time I saw Mom cry. I was amazed, first of all, that she was capable of tears. Second, I was amazed that she would shed them over someone so poisonous. Grandmother and I never had a moment of closeness; I couldn't remember one instance in which I felt loved or even accepted by her.

I was in junior high when Grandmother died, and I felt a moment of pure, unadulterated joy that was almost immediately mixed with guilt. I assuaged my guilt feelings by telling myself that Grandmother was in heaven with Jesus now, so it was okay to feel happy. In fact, I told myself, I feel happy on her behalf. My parents said Grandmother was sharing in the fellowship of the saints. They said she was experiencing eternal bliss. So I figured it was probably okay for me to dance around in the cemetery after her burial.

Chapter Ten

When I was about thirteen I started having dreams about flying. They always started out the same way: I dreamed that I was suddenly awake and it was the middle of the night in my bedroom. There I was in my cotton flannel nightgown, standing at my open window. The stars were bright; the night clear and warm. I rose up off my feet and floated out through the window, and then higher and higher. Up I floated, past the roof of our house, past the telephone wires, high into the sparkling night sky. I was exultant and completely happy. I swooped down, arms spread wide like wings, and began soaring over the tiny desert town and then over the western hills. My hair floated out behind me, the cool breeze in my face was exhilarating. I could go anywhere; I could do anything.

I flew past the town, past the wide stretches of desert, past Los Angeles and the coastal communities, to the Pacific Ocean. On the way I swooped down to brush the tops of trees with my hands as I flew past, and sometimes I flew close to the ground so I could look in the windows of city houses. Over the ocean I soared on the currents, sometimes turning over on my back so I could look up at the moon as I flew.

From there I visited different countries, and they were always so real, so intricate with detail. I stopped at special places and landed on the ground so I could get a better look. Whenever I saw a little girl I landed to see if I could talk to her, but usually she spoke some language I didn't understand.

The flying dreams returned, off and on, throughout the years, and in the periods where they didn't come I felt a deep sense of loss. Many times I prayed for them: "Please, dear God, let me have a flying dream tonight." They truly were the most wonderful things I ever experienced, whether in my waking or sleeping life, and I still yearn for them. Quite often I thought I was starting to have a flying dream but then I'd hit a ceiling or get tangled up in a tree and not be able to rise any farther.

I felt no fear in flying dreams, and they were the only time at night when fear was gone. I was still terrified of the dark. My parents, however, kept repeating that fear showed a lack of trust in God, so they didn't let me have a night-light or keep a lamp burning. According to them, I was supposed to glorify God by overcoming my fears. Sometimes I awakened screaming from a nightmare and they came into my room to ask what was wrong. Teeth chattering, head drenched in sweat, I could only say two words over and over: "Man coming. Man coming." They didn't like that. "There is no man coming. There's no man here but your dad. Stop acting up, and go to sleep."

It annoyed them that when I had nightmares my head perspired, drenching my pillow. I had to change the pillowcase every morning.

The only time in my life I can remember feeling truly safe was when I was nestled on Omma's lap, outside our little house in Korea. She was cross-legged on the ground, leaning back against the wall. I sat in the hollow of her lap, resting my head back against her chest, and her arms were wrapped around me. Her *hanbok* was old, well-worn cotton, shiny in some places, soft and enveloping. The sleeves were large, and she tucked her hands inside the opposite sleeve as she wrapped her arms around me so that it was an unbroken circle of soft fabric with her strong arms inside around my body. My knees were drawn up, and she tucked the fabric from the ends of her sleeves underneath my bare toes to keep me warm.

Wrapped that way I was like a little chrysalis in a tight-fitting cotton cocoon of safety and love. I could feel the rise and fall of her chest with her breathing. I knew that over the top of my head she was looking at the mountains. I focused on them as well, for a while, until my eyes grew heavy. Infused with a delicious sense of safety and peace and contentment, I fell asleep in her arms. And as I drifted off I could feel the soft butterfly kisses she pressed from time to time on the top of my head.

....

I have friends who can recall going to church as children, but none of them quite understand why religion looms so menacingly over all my memories. Of course, my parents were not like any others I have known; our household was not like any other Christian household I've encountered.

They were steely-eyed, fixed-smile zealots, of the mold that turns out martyrs and Crusaders. Satan was the enemy, followed closely by humanism. Personal rights were nonexistent. Horrible things could be done in the name of the Lord.

My parents were also automatons. They didn't speak, or apparently even think, anything that wasn't out of the Bible. Thinking independently was wrong, they said, because we were supposed to fill our minds and hearts so full of God's word that there wasn't room for any other thoughts, an idea I found profoundly claustrophobic.

"But, Dad, why do we believe everything in the Bible?" I would challenge, "What if things got written down wrong? What if people made stuff up?"

"The men who wrote the Bible were inspired by God, so everything in it is transferred directly from the mind of God to the hands of the men writing. We believe it in its entirety."

"Why?"

"Because God says to do so."

"But how do we know God really said that?"

"Because the Bible says He did."

Sometimes I got so frustrated by those senseless answers that I thought I'd scream. But since I wasn't allowed to even cry, let alone scream, I swallowed my anger and kept my face expressionless.

There we sat in the living room, three Bible-programmed robots. My parents sat in their chairs, and I sat curled up in the corner of the sofa, clenching the tassels of the throw pillows. Sometimes I imagined what would happen if I stood up and gave voice to my thoughts: "Why can't I think for myself? Why do you think you know everything? Maybe you don't know anything!"

And while I pondered how cataclysmic such a scene would be, Dad prayed aloud while Mom provided the background chorus.

"Dear Lord, forgive us for having any doubts about your holy word."

"Yes, dear Lord."

"And cleanse our minds and hearts of all worldly thoughts so that we can be holy, even as you are holy."

"Make it so, Jesus."

"And keep us from letting Satan get a foothold into our lives."

"Oh, we beg you, Lord."

"For you and you alone can save us. And we want to share in your suffering and in your shame so that we can someday share in your glory, and sit at your right hand."

"We do, Lord. Yes indeed."

"And create in Elizabeth a clean heart, and renew a right spirit within her."

"Oh mold her into a Christlike image, Lord."

Then it was my turn to pray, and the prayer had to be a certain length, with a definite fervor, and enough penitence and verbal self-flagellation to satisfy my parents so they'd let me go to bed.

"Dear Lord, please forgive me for questioning your holy word. Please forgive me for letting Satan give me any doubts about the Bible. Please forgive me for talking back to Dad and Mom and for being grumpy this morning. Help make me a better girl. For Jesus' sake, amen."

When I finally got in bed, away from my parents and away from the Bible, I felt an enormous sense of relief. In the darkness of my bedroom I could think my own thoughts—even if I was afraid they were blasphemous enough to send me to hell—and I could imagine and dream and retreat into my make-believe world.

In my make-believe world, the fantasies echoed the ones Omma and I shared: I escaped somehow and lived in a place that was green and hilly, where I had lots of friends and lots of love. In my favorite fantasy, a man came to the door and announced that my adoption was all a big misunderstanding: He was actually my real father and he'd been unable before now to come get me. He took me with him to England, where he had an estate in the countryside. He taught me how to ride horses, and there was a big garden. He had a cook and housekeeper who adored me. Every day I took afternoon tea in the garden with him, and eventually I grew up to become a famous Shakespearean actress.

....

Unfortunately, I would always wake up from these dreams, and if I was very unlucky, I'd wake up on Sunday.

On Sundays I got up at seven. Sunday school was at nine-thirty, and by the time I was in junior high I taught a Sunday school class. After breakfast and doing the dishes, I got ready for church and scanned my Sunday school lesson—I never spent the time preparing it that Dad thought I did, and by now his approval meant less and less to me.

I played piano for the "opening exercises," where all the Sunday school classes gathered together for fifteen minutes to sing songs and pray before going to their separate classrooms.

Then I took my little class of first- and second-graders into our room, where we played games for a while. I usually told them a story using felt cut-out figures on a felt background, and then I let them tell stories themselves and play with the felt people. Discipline was nonexistent, and I tried to keep the religious part of Sunday school to a bare minimum.

At ten-thirty Sunday school was over. Then I had to get into my choir robe, arrange the morning's music on the piano, and get ready for the church service. Every week I played a different prelude, usually something by Bach or Chopin, as people were gathering in the sanctuary. It always annoyed me that nobody paid any attention to something I'd worked on pretty hard throughout the week. During the service I sat at the piano, in full view of the congregation. That meant I had to look sweet and Christlike and interested in the sermon for the entire hour. As I got older I let the perfect facade drop every now and then, and sometimes I didn't bother about stifling my yawns or hiding my boredom.

After church there was usually "cookie hour," where I helped pour tea or coffee. I was always in the kitchen afterward, helping clean up. Somehow, Mom never managed to wash one dish.

It amazed me how much free labor the church got out of its members, especially its female members. A coterie of about ten women in our church worked like dogs, cooking and baking for church socials, washing dishes, arranging flowers, cutting and sewing quilts for missionaries. Nobody ever seemed too appreciative either. If you were a godly woman that kind of devotion was expected.

I snickered to myself over the competition between the women in the church for their pathetic crumbs of glory. Which cake the minister took seconds of, which casserole dish was scraped clean, which stack of sandwiches got placed in front of the others—all those things were life and death to the Women's Missionary Society.

Many of the women were very sweet, and some were nice to

me. One of them, a widow named Helen, treated me with a kindness I never received in my own home. In fact, I used to day-dream that Mom died—maybe killed by a migraine or some-thing—and Dad married Helen. We'd bake cookies together and she'd take me shopping, and she wouldn't punish me if the bed wasn't made with perfectly squared sheet corners.

I always wondered what Helen was doing in that church. She laughed loudly and often, and sometimes winked at me when the other women started arguing over whose flower arrange-ment to put on the pulpit. From time to time I heard the others whisper about Helen: She was a "loose" woman—I assume be-cause she went on weekend jaunts with friends and wore slacks and red lipstick to church and smoked cigarettes in the parking lot.

Once a year, on Mother's Day, the service was devoted to the women in the church. That meant the Bible reading was out of Proverbs: "A virtuous woman, who can find? For her price is far above rubies. The heart of her husband trusteth in her, and she does him good, and not ill . . ." Being a virtuous woman meant you worked hard, never complained, obeyed God and the men in your life, and kept yourself pure in body and mind.

For that you were rewarded with one service a year in your honor, where you could wear a white carnation and maybe get a bouquet of roses if you had given birth to more children than any of your sisters in the congregation. Then you served lunch and cleaned up afterwards.

....

I was told that being a godly woman began by being a godly child, and that meant saving souls as soon as possible.

According to my parents, if anyone I knew went to hell, I

would be held accountable. It was my duty to bring my friends to the Lord, and I knew that if I failed, they would suffer for eternity. Every evening after family Bible time, the same question was asked: "Have you brought your little friends to the Lord Jesus Christ? Because if they die without the Lord they will spend eternity in hell, and it will be your fault."

Talk about pressure: Now not only was it my job to make everyone around me happy and to make the Lord Jesus Christ proud of me and to please God and to please my parents, but the eternal salvation of everyone I knew rested on my shoulders.

One of the few kids who would have anything to do with me was a red-haired girl named Brenda. When I entered sixth grade the middle school was only a couple of miles away, so I started walking instead of riding the elementary school bus. We were in the same sixth-grade class and she lived two blocks away, so every day we walked to and from school together. I liked Brenda and I didn't want her to burn in the fires of hell for eternity, so I tried to save her soul.

One day after school I went to her house and we took glasses of Kool-Aid into her room. We sat on the bed and talked about various things, and I finally worked up my courage enough to blurt out: "Brenda, you're going to go to hell unless you accept Jesus Christ as your personal savior. Would you like to ask Jesus into your heart?"

Brenda sat on the bed in her culottes and sweater and stared at me. She told me her family was Jewish. She told me she wasn't interested.

I told her that her eternal soul was at stake.

I left a few minutes later—Brenda still unsaved—and went home. Our relationship was never the same. She avoided me after that and I walked to school by myself. My parents told me I should have tried harder. They said that at the Last Judgment, when "the last trumpet shall sound and the dead in Christ will rise first," I was going to have to go before God and explain to Him why Brenda was in hell and why I didn't bring her to the Lord. They took my guilt a step further, saying "her blood will be on your head."

Losing the one friend I had was heartbreaking. And trying to justify myself to my parents was impossible. They didn't care that she was Jewish—in fact, since she was one of "God's Chosen People" who had rejected the Messiah, saving her soul would have been considered even more of a coup.

Somehow I was supposed to have the power to bring everyone I knew to salvation. But how that belief dovetailed with the belief of predestination, I didn't know. And I never quite understood how it was my fault, if they were already predestined for hell anyway.

From time to time I asked tentatively about Buddhism, trying to find a shred of comfort over my mother. "Buddhism's a nice religion, don't you think? It's peaceful. It believes in being kind, just like Jesus. Don't you think it's possible that Buddhists might go to heaven?" Dad was always firm. "Buddhists will burn in hell for all eternity, just like everyone else who hasn't accepted Christ as their personal savior. Being nice or kind doesn't matter. The nicest and kindest of people are going to hell without Christ."

The contrast between my mother's Buddhism and my parents' fundamentalist Christianity was immeasurable. There was nothing you need do in one and endless work in the other. Omma never told me to believe anything; I could chant with her if I wanted or just play, I could meditate with her or just go to sleep. She simply was, and she let me simply be. If she believed in anything I think it was in the inherent rightness of life. I don't know if she believed in reincarnation; I don't know if she believed in God. She had her own little rituals that were for no one's comfort but her own.

My parents' faith required twenty-four hours a day vigilance. They read I Peter 5:8 to me: "Be on the alert. Your adversary, the devil, prowls about like a roaring lion, seeking someone to devour." Vigilance was required not only for our own souls but for those around us. The work was endless, and even your best efforts might not be enough. "Many are called," the Bible says, "but few are chosen."

On Saturdays I had to do "house-to-house visitation." Instead of staying home watching cartoons, I got up early and dressed as if I were going to church. A few diehard evangelical types met at the church at 8:00 A.M. for coffee and strategy. Dad, who was by this time the church's minister, led the attack.

With the street plan map laid out on the table, we gathered around and planned how to divide our small town and conquer. Then we held hands and prayed, asking God to touch people's hearts and prepare fertile soil for our eventual sowing of "the seed of the Lord's word." When I was a teenager I started changing the prayer to "the seed of the Lord" just to amuse myself. Nobody ever seemed to find anything odd about my phraseology.

Then we fanned out. My dad and I always went together, driving in the dilapidated yellow church van. To me, a successful morning of house-to-house visitation was when no one answered their doors. I held my breath as we walked up to each house, silently chanting my Saturday-morning mantra: "pleasedon'tbe-homepleasedon'tbehome." It was awful when the door was opened. It was beyond awful when another kid opened the door. Holding my Bible in my sweaty hands, I said my lines: "Hi there. How are you today? I'm here to invite you to attend a service at our church." We were trained in exactly how to respond to whatever the person said.

"I'm already a member of a church."

"Great! Which one? Because it's important that your church teach the Word of God in its entirety and that it teaches redemption through Jesus Christ."

"I'm not interested."

"Really? Are you interested in being able to choose between eternal damnation and eternal glory at the right hand of God? Because without Christ, you're doomed for eternity."

"Get the hell off my property."

"Harden not your heart against the Lord, my friend."

If my dad wasn't within earshot I simply invited them to church, apologized for bothering them, and got away as quickly as possible.

Maybe one visit a month would actually "bear fruit," as the little band of soul-savers called it. Occasionally someone would actually accept the invitation and come to church the next Sunday.

....

The big problem I had all my life with fundamentalist Christianity is that it contradicts itself. It makes no sense. Even at that age I couldn't reconcile the conflicting teachings: "The heart is deceitful and, above all things, desperately wicked," on one hand, and "Man was made in the image of God," on the other. So I wondered: Did that mean that the heart of God is deceitful and above all things desperately wicked? Maybe so.

And there was the theory of predestination coming in direct conflict with evangelical fervor. Also, the things in the Bible that we took literally and lived by were, it seemed to me, so arbitrarily chosen, especially with regard to the Old Testament. There were so many rules laid down there, and we obviously didn't live by all of them.

For example, when women were menstruating they weren't forced to leave the confines of the city, as they were in biblical times. But there were certain things in the Old Testament, especially about homosexuality, that fundamentalist Christians absolutely embraced. So who decided which things in the Old Testament were valid and which were nullified by the death of Jesus Christ? My parents told me that blood sacrifices no longer had to be made as they were in the Old Testament because when Christ came He was the once and forever sacrifice for sins. Okay, I thought, great. But there were other things in the Old Testament that we still followed, and many we didn't. Who made the rules?

Another thing that really bothered me was the teaching of Paul in the New Testament. I disliked him when I was a child, and the feeling grew as I got into my teens. Paul, I thought, was a misogynistic, hateful, judgmental lunatic. I could never understand my parents' reverence for Paul. And my parents would rationalize some of the things he said, such as his rule that women were to keep silent. Well, the women in our church certainly didn't keep silent, least of all Mom. So even though I thought Paul's entire philosophy was nonsensical, I couldn't understand why—if we followed the New Testament in toto—we didn't follow that.

My parents said that Paul was talking to a certain kind of woman at a particular time in which there were big problems. But the same could be said of any of the teachings from the Bible. No matter how you sliced it, it didn't make sense. It never flowed in a logical manner. Whenever I'd get to that point in the argument, Dad would say we had to accept it by faith.

And so I did. Even though fundamentalist Christianity was

the absolute epitome to me of illogical, muddled thinking, I accepted everything on faith. The fear factor was so intense that even though I couldn't embrace it wholeheartedly, I did the best I could so that I wouldn't spend eternity in a lake of fire being tormented by legions of Satan's demons.

....

There was no escape from the watchful eye of God. Religion permeated absolutely every area of our lives. Even something as simple as going out to McDonald's became a trial by fire.

I hated going out to meals with my parents because we always had to pray before we ate. It made no difference whether we were out in public or at home, Dad talked just as loudly, prayed just as eloquently, and we held hands and my face burned with embarrassment. Everyone in the restaurant stared. We lived in a tiny town, so wherever we went I always saw someone I knew. And of course they snickered, and I was mortified, and my parents said it was an honor to be shamed because of Christ.

That was another quandary for me. Why was wearing a badge of shame something to be so proud of? "Praise God," my parents said, "if people ridicule or revile you for the Lord's sake."

For example, the clothing and hairstyle I was forced to wear were so out of style. But when I said anything, my parents said I should be proud to be ashamed for Christ and share in His suffering.

Although how Christ was glorified by me having to wear an ugly dress was never explained.

....

Not only was I terrified of God, I was terrified of His house as well. I hated church buildings, and was ashamed of feeling that way—after all, it was the temple of God. Our sanctuary was laid out in a simple pattern: two sections of pews, the altar at the front, then behind that the platform and the baptistery. The sanctuary smelled dank and dusty. The woodwork was shiny from being rubbed by so many hands over so many years, and the burgundy pew cushions were frayed and lumpy.

Every Sunday, after the morning worship service, it was my job to go down the aisles and collect trash people left behind, straighten up the hymn books, and make everything spic and span. If it was communion Sunday, there were about a hundred tiny communion glasses, with their residue of grape juice, to be washed and dried. The cracker wafers and grape juice represented the body and blood of the Lord.

Sometimes, if no one was looking, I'd take a swig of Welch's grape juice right out of the bottle. I felt about as bad as could be, but exhilarated and dangerous too. I told my one friend: "Hey, you know what I did today? I chugged the blood of the Lord, man."

....

The one part of church I liked was hymn singing. Many of them were profoundly comforting to me, and I sang them over and over to myself:

> *When peace, like a river*
> *Attendeth my way;*
> *When sorrows like sea billows roll:*
> *Whatever my lot, Thou hast taught me to say*
> *"It is well, it is well, with my soul."*

Fundamentalist Christians "wrestle in prayer," which means they pray and pray and pray until they feel they have an answer.

I did that a lot: on my knees, pounding at the door of heaven. I wanted the peace everybody said the Lord could give. I wanted to know I was saved. I wanted to feel the Holy Ghost filling me up.

> *Be near me, Lord Jesus, I ask Thee to stay*
> *Close by me forever, and love me, I pray.*
> *Bless all the dear children in Thy tender care*
> *And fit us for heaven to live with Thee there.*

I never understood how Jesus—so gentle, so compassionate—could allow such suffering of the children in His tender care. The only explanation I could come up with was that God the Father was the one who really called the shots, and Jesus, while the Son of God, actually had very little power. All the love, but little of the power.

Evidence of the severity of Almighty God was constantly before me. The Heavenly Father I knew was a God of wrath. He was the one who turned Lot's wife into a pillar of salt simply because she looked back over her shoulder at her city. He was the one who forced a father to sacrifice his daughter simply to teach him a lesson. He was the one who destroyed an entire world with a flood and saved only Noah's family. He was the one who took Omma from me.

....

For a child, God's will manifested itself through the rules of the parents. As a wife, God's will manifested itself through the wishes of the husband. In any case, a female, and especially a female child, had no rights whatsoever. In that respect, my American life was no different from Omma's life in Korea.

I was given no leeway in that household. In season or out of season, rain or shine, sick or healthy, there were certain things I was expected to do. When I was twelve and had stomach flu I asked Mom if I could go to bed early that night. I felt queasy and weak. She told me I wasn't going to bed until after the supper dishes had been cleaned and put away and the kitchen swept, as usual. I told her I was really sick and I didn't think I could stand at the sink and do the dishes.

Since my primary goal in life was to please my parents and please God and thus avoid getting sent back to the orphanage and/or going to hell, I hoped that Mom would believe me. I never tried to get out of my work. I rarely complained about anything. I never asked for anything—it would never have occurred to me to ask. But she was unyielding.

So I stood at the sink, doing the dishes, feeling hot and sick the whole time. I just managed to get the last dish washed and in the drainer when I began to throw up. There was nothing I could do to stop it. I threw up all over the sink and the clean dishes and the counter. Mom was enraged; she saw it as deliberate evil and rebelliousness.

Not only was I spanked severely, but I had to clean up the mess and rewash all the dishes and scrub down the kitchen with Lysol before I could go to bed.

....

There was a piece of musical flotsam called "Sunday School Song" that my parents loved. They thought it would "appeal to the young folks." I was one of the young folks, and I knew it was crap. But they wanted me to perform it at youth group conventions. They had visions of me traveling all over the country, an inspiring young Asian American musical evangelist, singing

"Sunday School Song" in front of clean-living Christian teens. I begged and begged, but they were implacable.

So I performed it—complete with the peppy movements that illustrated the verses. I made an unutterable fool of myself. I stood on stage, sweating and trembling, wishing I'd have a heart attack and die or Armageddon would begin—anything to put an end to my misery. I hated my parents for putting me through that torture.

The tune was idiotic; the words were drivel:

Come to the Sunday School and have a lot of fun.
Old folks, young folks, everybody come.

And that was just the chorus. There were several stanzas, each recounting some story out of the Bible in nauseatingly coy verse.

After the first performance I told my parents how stupid the song was, how much I hated it, and how humiliated I felt. Dad was shocked by my attitude.

"You mean to tell me that Jesus was willing to die for your sins, but you're not willing to sing a song for him? And he was mocked and ridiculed and made to wear a crown of thorns, and you're complaining about something like this? You know, the Bible says to make your salvation sure. I think you better do some praying about your own salvation. You get down on your knees and tell Jesus that you don't love him enough to sing a little song for him."

Oh, puleeze, I thought.

"I'm sorry," I said.

I had to perform in church nearly every week, either singing a solo or playing something on the piano. My parents never seemed to like what I did, but they kept pushing me to do it

Sunday after Sunday. I waited on the car ride home from church for something approaching a compliment, but that never came.

Sometimes I asked. "Was the solo okay?" The answer was never what I wanted.

"Well, your voice sounded thin and you didn't make much eye contact with the audience. And why didn't you play the Bach during offertory? Did you practice those pieces this week?"

I always ended up apologizing. "I know. I didn't do a very good job. I'm sorry."

My parents would glance at each other and shake their heads, and we'd finish the car ride home in silence.

Chapter Eleven

In our tiny town, I stuck out like a sore thumb. The kids in junior high school had a name for what I was: gook. I had one friend, Lenore, who was also ostracized, but for a different reason—she was too smart for a girl. She liked science and math; she planned to get a Ph.D. In a town where the ultimate fantasy of pre-pubescent girls was to marry the high school quarterback and go on weekly shopping trips to Sears, she was nothing less than a freak.

I met Lenore in the school lunchroom on the first day of seventh grade. She was sitting by herself, reading. I walked past her to get to an empty seat and she looked up and smiled. "You smell good," she said. "And your hair is so wild and cool." I was thunderstruck—that was the first time anyone had ever complimented me on my appearance.

I sat down by her and within five minutes we were chatting away, making acerbic comments about the haughty, witless crowd around us.

To me, Lenore was perfect. She had blond hair and sky-blue eyes. She made fun of her long "stork legs" and her straight hair. I thought I'd cut off my right arm for either. She said I was interesting and funny and brilliant. She said I was pretty and "exotic"-looking. I worshipped her.

On my first day of junior high school one of the eighth-grade boys announced to the lunchroom: "Hey, did you know gooks have two pussies? That's because they're all whores and they're all poor, so they can do two guys at once." The lunchroom exploded in laughter.

For the rest of my junior-high time, the label stayed with me. Someone even wrote about it in my eighth-grade yearbook: "To a pretty cool gook, even if she does have two you-know-whats." Lenore dismissed that with one withering comment. "She's a moron," Lenore said. "She's not worth worrying about."

....

I had managed to find a girlfriend, but boys were another story. In seventh grade, I got a tremendous crush on a boy who was a senior in high school and was president of our church youth group. I was obsessed by books, so I assumed the things that moved me would move other people as well. At the time I was reading *Little Women,* and I was enamored of Jo. I thought Beth was a milquetoast and Amy was a snotty bitch and Margaret was an affected prig, but Jo was perfect. Jo had kind of a breezy way of talking, and I assumed that because I liked her so much, anybody I liked would be impressed by how much I resembled her.

Ironically, the boy I liked was named Joe. It seemed too perfect.

So one Saturday we all went on an outing to an observatory and I got to go along even though I wasn't part of the youth group, because Dad was leading the expedition. I dressed with special care, and when I saw him, I adopted my best Jo March voice and used her lingo: "Dear Joe, what ho?" He looked blankly at me, turned around and began talking to a tall, blond sixteen-year-old beauty, and ignored me for the rest of the day. In fact, from then on he steered clear of me as much as he possibly could.

Looking back, I can see why he would, how uncomfortable and embarrassed he must have been, and how weird he must have thought I was. But at the time, it crushed me. I couldn't understand how he could turn away from me when I quoted Louisa May Alcott. How could that be?

....

In our little desert town, everyone knew everyone else. I hated that.

I knew that anything I did at school would be reported to my parents, and the good minister's daughter role was so tough to keep up. At church I did everything that was expected of me. I taught Sunday school, I took care of music for the worship services, I typed up the Sunday morning bulletins. I smiled and prayed and—when I was in the midst of it—really did believe what was being said.

When I got into high school, things changed. I let my grades slip and I talked to my teachers with bored sarcasm. I told my English teacher she was a bitch; I spent lots of time in the principal's office. But the kids didn't make fun of me anymore. Now I was the smart-ass preacher's kid, not the weird goody-goody gook. Kids laughed at my jokes instead of my face. I had finally found a way to gain acceptance.

My parents were angry and disappointed with me, even though they didn't know the half of it. What they did know was that my report cards weren't all As anymore, and I got detention slips on a regular basis.

Dad lectured me over and over about it, and about the disrespectful way I talked to mother. "Honor your father and your mother, that your days may be long upon this earth," he reminded me. "She's not my mother," I snapped back. That earned me a hard slap across my face and confinement to my room, where at least I could think my own thoughts and whisper to myself my contempt for their incessant hypocrisy.

About that time, my feelings about Mom crystallized, moving from fear to contempt. I saw her as smug and hypocritical, and I called her "the Martyr," which sent Dad into a rage. On the shelf in Dad's library was a copy of Fox's *Book of Martyrs*, a book that details the suffering of various Christians down through the years who died for their beliefs. One day when Mom told me I had a bad attitude and should read a chapter from it every day I answered, "Okay. I'll start with the chapter about you."

Mom spent most of her time lying on the sofa, wanly complaining of migraine. She told me not to be so loud with the vacuuming. She told Dad to punish me for giving her "hurtful" looks. She told me I was lazy and spent too much time reading.

She reminisced about growing up: She was such a popular teenager that for her sixteenth birthday her parents threw a gala party and hired an orchestra.

She often compared herself to me: Her legs were long, mine were short; her hair had golden glints in it, mine was dull; she had lots of beaus in her teens, I had none; she was a coloratura soprano opera singer in her twenties, I had an unexciting alto voice.

Mom viewed me as free help; she didn't have to pay me but I did all the housework—cleaning, cooking, laundry. I gave her neck and back rubs when she had headaches. I seethed inside, but I did it. On weekday mornings I got up early so I'd have time to wash the breakfast dishes before leaving for school. Mom checked to make sure the beds were made perfectly, with squared corners and top sheets folded back evenly over the blankets.

When I got home I had an hour of practicing on the piano, then dinner to cook and the kitchen to clean. After that I finished my homework and we gathered in the living room for our evening Bible study.

But the day of the week I really began to hate was Sunday. There were two church services at least, and usually some church social. I helped out in the kitchen at church potlucks, washing the remains of Jell-O salad off greasy plates. The food at potlucks was vile. One woman came up to me and said patronizingly, "Dear, I made this dish especially for you: It's Oriental casserole. It's got ground beef and Chun King crunchy noodles and mushroom soup in it." You stupid bitch, I thought, smiling and thanking her, all the while picturing myself shoving the nauseating concoction in her face.

Clearly, there were mixed feelings about me in our otherwise pure-white congregation. I got barbed comments from time to time. "I hope you thank God every day that your wonderful mom and dad took you out of that awful country." "Goodness, I don't know how those Oriental folks eat the awful stuff they do. Aren't you lucky to get good American food."

Once a black couple came to church on Sunday morning, and the tension in the sanctuary was palpable as they walked up the center aisle to find seats in an empty pew. The church was filling up, but no one sat in the same pew as the couple—they were in complete isolation on that long stretch of pine.

Fortunately for the church's sensibilities, the couple was just in town visiting. Newcomers to church were always asked to stand at the beginning of the morning service and "tell us a little something" about themselves. The couple stood up, smiled shyly, and said they were from Indiana and were in the area vacationing. You could almost hear the sighs of relief from throughout the congregation.

After church the couple left immediately—ducking out under cover of the closing hymn—and people began talking. "Why would a colored couple come here? Why didn't they find a church with their own kind?"

Mom said she wasn't racist, but it did seem just a little odd that they'd choose a church full of white people to visit. Years later the church became "integrated." There were one Hispanic family and one black family that attended sporadically, but neither was really involved in church activities.

In the meantime, most people at church were civil but chilly to them. Many people completely ignored them. I told my parents that the attitude of people toward this family was despicable.

Mom was incensed. "I'm not a bit racist," she said. "When that colored woman came up to me after church and wanted to give me a hug I let her."

Mom and I argued quite often about that topic. I said that she and pretty much everyone else in the church was racist. Didn't Jesus love everyone the same? What made Mom better than someone with darker skin?

Her attitude pretty much summed up the rest of the church's: Jesus may have died for everyone, but that didn't mean we had to mingle with them.

"Colored folks are different but I've got nothing against them," Mom said. "When I was a girl we had the nicest colored lady for years who cleaned the house. When she was sick we gave her a pot of soup to take home. You're just a troublemaker."

....

My bad attitude finally started to wear so much on my parents that they took me to a Christian therapist. "He's a godly man," they said. "He's not a regular humanist psychiatrist."

He had no credentials, but that didn't matter: His office was in a church building, he wore a tiny gold cross on his suit lapel, and the requisite saccharine smile was stamped on his face.

I went to him because, my parents said, I was rebelling against them and against the Lord. They were sick and tired of my lack of respect. They'd had enough of my moods. Christ Himself was starting to wonder if I really wanted to be saved.

So on Friday afternoons I sat in a cramped, sweltering office on a molded plastic chair while this man pontificated about Christ and the Teen Years. He was in his mid-fifties, short and paunchy, balding and smooth-skinned.

There was precious little therapy at work—as soon as he asked me a question, he answered it himself.

"Now just why is it you feel your parents don't really love you?" he asked.

132

"Well, they always tell me what a disappointment I was, and—"

"Just a doggone minute. I'm sure they say no such thing. They just want you to be grateful. You were a godless little orphan, and you haven't always acted like a very nice girl. God has been so very good to you. You don't deserve any of the things God has given you, because you're a sinner in His sight. But through the mercy of Jesus Christ you've been given a chance at salvation."

Silence.

"So why do you still cry over your birth mother?"

"What are you, stupid or something? Why do you think I cry? Because she's my mother and I—"

"Whoa! Let's hold it right there, miss. You don't use that kind of language in the Lord's house. Satan has his foothold in you, and you crucify the Lord Jesus afresh every time you talk like that."

Then he'd lay his sweaty palm on my knee and massage it while he prayed for me.

When I became an adult and started seeing a real therapist I decided to tell my parents about it. During one of our weekly phone conversations I broached the subject, not quite sure how they'd respond.

Their first question was the same one they asked about everyone I ever mentioned: "Is she a Christian?"

I told them I had no idea, but I doubted it.

"If you're going to talk to anyone, it should be a Christian," they told me. "Remember that wonderful man we took you to in your teens? He was so Christlike. He straightened you out right quick."

They told me prayer, not therapy, was the answer.

And anyway, so what if I was suffering? We suffer with Christ, therefore we can reign with Christ.

Suffering was the whole point.

....

While I finally gained a precarious measure of acceptance in high school, I never got asked out on a date. Being friends with me was one thing, but anything more than that was off-limits in our town. I had a crush on one boy in my drama group, and we spent lots of time together, talking about life and philosophy and movies.

I wasn't allowed to go to movies, so he described each new release in great detail, and it was almost as good as seeing it myself. He only talked to me after drama group, though, when other kids weren't around. Finally one day I mustered up all my courage and invited him to the school's Sadie Hawkins Day dance. He was visibly embarrassed. "I'm really sorry, but I can't. I like you and all, but my parents would never let me date a gook."

I was devastated. During our long conversations I had almost forgotten I was a gook; I had just felt like a normal teenage girl. We never talked after drama group again.

....

The only reality that I wanted any part of was found in literature. The noble suffering of the poets was all that gave me hope. There had to be something to cling to in this world, if Tennyson could say:

> *Let the sweet heavens endure,*
> *Not close and darken above me*

Before I am quite quite sure
That there is one to love me;
Then let come what may
To a life that has been so sad,
I shall have had my day.

I spent most of my spare time with my nose in a book. I wasn't allowed to read most novels or magazines, but I preferred early British writers anyway. My daydreams weren't of rock stars or actors but of Fitzwilliam Darcy and Robert Browning.

I trembled when I read Herrick's paeans of love and lust to Julia, and a riot of feelings surged within me when I read about the glories of her naked body in the river, and her hair, and her breasts. If I had to be born at all it should have been in a different place and time, I told myself; I should be walking with a breeches-clad gentleman in Kentish fields, wearing a tight bodice and full silk skirt.

I wanted to go to college and study English literature, but I didn't know where the money would come from. It didn't occur to me to expect my parents to foot the bill. Besides, I knew my parents wanted me to do one of two things: become a missionary or get married and become a godly wife.

My high school English teacher—who also doubled as the school's drama coach—had high hopes for me. She told me I should pursue a career that took me out of the little town and maybe even set my sights on writing. She told me she didn't want me to end up like most of the other school graduates would—married, settled down in the same town they'd grown up in, working at some unimaginative job. "You deserve better than this," she said. "You've got extraordinary talent and character. Don't throw it away."

There was part of me that believed her, but it was weak. If

she was telling me the truth—that I was a brilliant girl, that I could do something wonderful with my life—then why didn't anyone else see it?

Her belief in me echoed Omma's belief, but it was too frightening to contemplate that maybe those two women were right, and everyone else was wrong. It was easier just to think that she, like Omma, had some inexplicable affection for me that blinded her to my essential worthlessness.

I didn't do much planning about my life after high school. I was so tired and so discouraged that even my rebelliousness diminished. My grades were mediocre, except in English and music. I frittered away time and energy fantasizing about freedom but didn't know how to take the steps to achieve it. I waited for something to intervene, and when that happened it wasn't at all what I'd dreamed.

Section

III

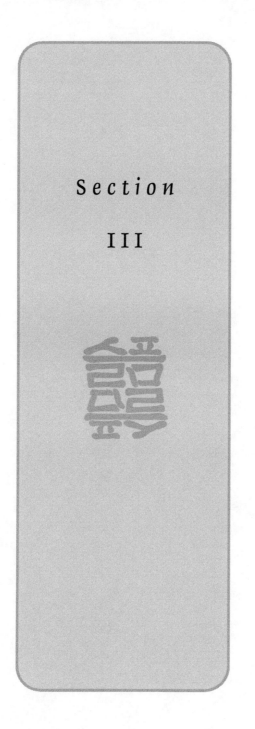

In my dying there could be an awakening
Or in my dying there could be just dying.
The problem is I have no way to know
And I want to know everything.
Like what's inside the shining center of my soul
And whether anyone loves me
And what's beyond the realm of dreams
And what small creatures think about
And if I'm worth the pain I cause myself.
This moment passes just like the last
And the next is forgotten at its birth.
But oh, how strong the longing is
To step outside this fragile heart
And touch the heart of darkness
and light, and end, and beginning.
If love were here, would I want to leave?
I don't have an answer.
I just know that love has never made itself at home with me
And all it's ever been is a mystery
Longing, ache.
And life's worn out its welcome.
I still care about the world
And care so deeply
That I'm hanging on the cross of my construction
Weeping with despair
That even in death I find
No redemption or salvation
For myself or any other.

Chapter Twelve

I got married on a Saturday morning in our church. Dad walked me down the aisle and then officiated at the ceremony. My new husband was a deacon in our church. I was seventeen, just graduated from high school.

My parents had pretty much chosen D. for me late in my senior year. They invited him to visit a few times and questioned him closely. He had the same conservative, fundamentalist beliefs they did, and they wanted me to be married to a "godly man" as soon as possible. My parents believed that a Christian marriage—not a career or education or personal fulfillment—was the highest calling a woman could have. D. believed everything my parents believed: that the Bible was the word of God; that husbands were to be dominant over their wives; that I needed harsh discipline.

I fell in with their wishes and even daydreamed that maybe things would turn out magically—D. would love me and be kind to me, I'd be a good and sexy and obedient wife, we'd have a happy family. I never really thought I could do anything special, anyway, no matter what my English teacher and Omma had said. I felt pretty lucky that anyone even wanted to marry me.

On the night before the wedding, D. took me out to dinner. We weren't physically affectionate with each other, but I thought maybe that would change after we were married. I thought he was just being chaste, as a good Christian should. But I could feel the fear prickling the edge of my consciousness, warning me: This man never kisses you; this man's eyes are cold as ice. So as he was dropping me off at my parents' house, shortly before 9:00 P.M., I asked him, "Do you love me?" There was silence, then he reached over across me and opened my car door. "I'm marrying you tomorrow," he said. "So don't ask stupid questions."

I went inside and crawled into bed, and the full force of what was about to happen hit me: I was going into another form of slavery. I had escaped being an indentured servant in Korea and being forced into a loveless marriage, and here it was happening in America. But was I being forced? I thought about going into my parents' room and telling them I couldn't marry this man, that I was terrified of him, that there was something inhuman in the icy way he stared at me and the flat tone of his voice.

Nobody could actually make me get married.

But the thought of what repercussions there would be was overwhelming. The wedding was set for 10:00 A.M. the next morning. The church was decorated and all its members planned to be there. Could I really stand up against that kind of pressure? I'd spent the past several years bowing to the wishes of my parents and the church. And now I was contemplating telling everyone that the foreign orphan who was adopted by their dearly loved pastor was going to disappoint him yet again. I just simply couldn't do it.

I got married in a dress I had made. It was white satin, with a modest train. The bodice had rose-patterned lace overlaid on the satin and long sleeves. I cut some roses out of the lace and appliquéd them on the skirt of the dress, and made a veil that gathered at the crown with a little cluster of roses I made out of the satin and lace. Nobody told me I looked beautiful, but I didn't expect it. Mom only remarked that the dress seemed awfully low cut for a wedding.

The church was full, but my English teacher wasn't there. The gift she sent, which arrived a few days after the wedding, was unusual: not a kitchen gadget or sheets or towels, but a gift certificate in my name to a bookstore. The card she sent read simply "Don't forget how special you are."

I walked down the aisle with Dad, who then turned around and officiated at the ceremony. D. didn't look at me. Dad read from the Bible: "Wives, obey your husbands, and be subject unto them as unto the Lord," and then I repeated the vow: "I take thee to be my lawfully wedded husband. To have and to hold, from this day forward. For better, for worse; for richer, for poorer; in sickness and in health; to honor and to obey; till death us do part."

After the ceremony there was a reception at the church, where we had punch and cake and everyone told me what a lucky girl I was. About an hour later, we went home. There was no honeymoon. We rode in silence to the house he had rented while he was building a new one, and when we got there I began unpacking my things, which I'd brought over the day before.

The first time D. struck me was later that day. We went to bed a couple of hours after we got home, because D. said that God expected a couple to "honor him in the marriage bed," even though there'd been no affection or caresses between us. But when D. couldn't consummate our marriage, I was punished. "This is your fault," he told me. "It's because of you." He slapped me as I lay, naked, on the bed, and while I looked at up him in shock he began punching me rhythmically. A few minutes later he was suddenly able to have sex. I was too stunned to think clearly, but a strong instinct for self-preservation kept me quiet and calm. After he fell asleep I went into the bathroom and curled up on the floor, pressing the cold tile against my hot face and my aching ribs.

The next day was Sunday, and we went to church, where D. took his place at the podium with Dad. D. read the Bible and said the opening prayer, and I played the piano for the service, as usual. People congratulated us and shook our hands, and I smiled.

We lived in a house D. built, with furniture he picked out. I kept the house immaculately clean, and I made food to his specifications. When I failed, the punishment was swift. A few days after our marriage I made a ratatouille—I didn't know at the time that D. hated zucchini. He took one bite, then picked up the casserole dish and tossed it out the dining room window.

The patio was covered in food, shards of glass from the window, and pieces of the stoneware casserole dish. I spent most of the night on my hands and knees outside, picking up every sliver, until I was ribboned with cuts.

I took the ice cubes out of a pitcher of orange juice he was trying to chill, and he pinned me against the refrigerator, punching my abdomen and ribs and then choking me until I lost consciousness and slumped down on the kitchen floor.

Everything I did was wrong. D. would erupt in rage in a split second, without warning, and no matter how hard I tried to keep things peaceful, I never succeeded. There was a book at the time called *The Total Woman*, and I decided to give its suggestions a try. I was as docile as possible. I agreed with everything he said. I shoved my own desires so far out of the way that I almost forgot what they were. Nothing helped.

The root problem—and the one I had no control over—was the way I looked. He hated it, and he took it as a personal affront. I could never figure out why he married me. Maybe it was so he'd have a constant focus for his anger.

We watched *The Elephant Man* one night on television. During a scene where the character has his face covered in cloth, D. turned to me and said, "Maybe you should do that." When I looked in the mirror for most of my life I saw a face as grotesque and misshapen as that of the "elephant man." I saw my wide cheekbones as a slab, my small nose as a flat blob, my eyes as tiny dark slits.

My body I saw as short and squat and revolting, littered with scars. My hair was a tangled, frizzy mop. I could see not one redeeming quality, nothing but ugliness through and through. So I ironed my hair, to make it lie flat. I dieted, to make my curvy body more bony and angular.

....

D. wanted a dog, and I was thrilled at the idea of finally getting to keep a pet. I didn't show a whole lot of enthusiasm, however—I had learned that the happier I seemed about something, the less inclined D. was to let me do it. So I kept quiet, and one day he came home with a collie puppy.

She was a golden, velvety bundle of uncomplicated love. She followed me around the house during the day, wagging and jumping up and sounding off with insistent little barks every few minutes. I vacuumed, and she growled at the light on the base of the vacuum and wrestled with the cord. I dusted, and she tried to tug the dust cloth out of my hands. I cooked and baked, and she ran around in circles in an ecstasy of anticipation. I house-trained her, dashing outside with her whenever the moment looked propitious and praising her lavishly.

When she and I were home alone together she was completely indulged, but D. was almost as strict with her as he was with me, and I think her spirits dropped along with mine at the sound of his car in the driveway at the end of the day.

One cold, windy February night she was cuddled up beside me on the floor, where I was hemming a pair of D.'s work pants. The house was clean and warm; I'd washed and dried the dinner dishes, and it was nearing bedtime.

Every night I hated putting her outside in the cold, even though she had a roomy redwood shingle doghouse with a scrap piece of carpet that was left over from our living room. But D. was adamant that the dog didn't sleep in the house.

On this particular night, however, I was brave enough—or stupid enough—to argue. "Can't she stay inside tonight? It's so cold outside and she's sleeping so comfortably. I'll let her out first thing in the morning. Please?"

He gave me that level stare and didn't answer. I went back to my hemming, hands shaking now. D. turned off the television and sat in his chair, motionless, just looking at me.

When D. was about to punish me for something, his body got

very still and his voice took on a soft, singsong quality. I could read the signs by now, of course, and I knew something terrible was coming. "You know what? Doghouses are for dogs to sleep in. So here's what you'll do: You'll both spend the night outside in the doghouse."

He opened the sliding glass door that led onto the porch. The dog—as schooled in obedience as I was—reluctantly went out, tail and head hanging down. I folded D.'s pants and laid them on the arm of his chair, put the needle and thread back in my wicker sewing basket and put it away in the hall closet, and put on my coat. I didn't say anything. There was nothing to say.

The dog and I crawled inside the A-frame redwood shingled doghouse, and I curled up around her soft, furry body. She licked my face and snuggled close against me, and we fell asleep.

The next morning the sliding glass door was unlocked, and I went inside and fixed D.'s breakfast.

Our roles were very clearly defined: D. told me what he wanted, and I obeyed. I kept the house clean. I did the cooking and laundry. I picked up after him—and it had to be immediately. I followed him around the bedroom as he undressed and picked up each sock and shirt as he tossed it to the floor.

We watched the television shows he chose, but I was allowed to sit down and watch only if the dinner dishes had been washed and dried and the kitchen was clean. He didn't like me to read, so I had to sneak moments here and there with my beloved books when he wasn't looking.

D. insisted that I keep busy. Whenever he was home he wanted to see me vacuuming or scrubbing the floors or dusting. When he left for work he checked the house; he checked again upon his return to make sure I'd actually made things cleaner than they were before.

He made plant holders out of chain that he soldered together; he put his photography up on the walls. Everything had to be kept the way he left it. Something as simple as moving an ice cube tray would send him into a rage.

After we had been married about a year, D. was diagnosed with paranoid schizophrenia, and he spent some time in the psychiatric ward of a hospital. It wasn't the violence at home that led to his hospitalization but rather problems he was having concentrating at work. He wanted to be a success and he often said everyone was against him, so he agreed to the treatment. As far as I know, his boss was the only one who encouraged him to get help—neither his family nor my parents acknowledged that there was anything wrong.

I drove down to see him every day. I was the dutiful, supportive wife. That two-week period was the best time in my marriage, because he wasn't home at all, and I could leave after visiting with him for an hour. But when he came home, it was as if nothing had changed. He stopped taking his medication; he said his psychiatrist was out to get him and he canceled his treatment; he quit his job and went to work at a business his family owned. The respite was over.

We told people at church that he had been out of town helping out family members, and everyone believed it. Women at church would tell me what a wonderful man he was and how good the Lord had been to me. "Look at you," one choir member told me. "You have everything you could ever want."

We had a nice new house with wall-to-wall carpeting, two cars, a boat, and a truck. We had several bank accounts, although I didn't know what was in them. I had no money of my own; D. said I didn't need any. We went grocery shopping together and he controlled what was purchased. I wasn't allowed to buy anything without his approval. I didn't write any of the checks. If I had to buy something, like gasoline, he gave me money and I gave him the change.

I'd been married about a year when I got pregnant. D. was furious. He had told me not to get pregnant until he decided it was time, and I was on birth control pills. But I stopped taking them without telling him. It was wrong, I know. It's wrong to have a child in that way or for those reasons. I felt tremendous guilt about the whole thing.

But oh, God, I was so lonely. I yearned for somebody to love. I ached to hold another human being and look at a face that looked back at mine tenderly, without revulsion. And I wanted someone who looked like me. I wanted to give my love to a person who had the same blood, the same features, as I did.

I didn't need to tell him I was pregnant. He knew when I missed my period. He kept exact track of everything about me. I wasn't even allowed to close the door when I used the bathroom. He kept count of how many tampons I used a month.

When I was pregnant, I tried to protect my stomach as much as possible from him. I was in love with the child inside me and immediately began spinning fantasies about what our lives would be like if we could just be alone together.

I knew from the first that I was carrying a daughter. I longed for that mother-daughter connection. The women at church said they knew by the way I was carrying it that the baby was a boy, but I knew differently. Mother and daughter: That's the way it had to be.

When D. was at work I talked to my child constantly. I told her what I was doing: "Don't be afraid, sweetheart, if you feel all topsy-turvy right now. I'm bending over to wash the floor. But everything's okay. I'm just taking you for a little roller-coaster ride." I stroked my belly and sang to the baby inside: "You are my sunshine, my only sunshine. You make me happy when skies are gray." I sat in the rocking chair and read poetry to her: "That was Donne, sweetheart. Now I'm going to read you Amy Lowell."

When I was about six months pregnant, I suffered from terrible morning sickness and couldn't get out of bed to fix D.'s breakfast. We had one of those '70s waterbeds that was placed directly on the floor, inside a wooden frame.

D. was standing beside the bed in his work boots and khaki pants, and he didn't say anything when I told him I was too sick to get up. He just looked at me.

Then he jumped from the floor onto my stomach and left for work.

During my pregnancy D. went to natural childbirth classes with me, and people in the church were impressed. The perfect husband, doing the perfect thing. I wanted Leigh to be born without any anesthetic in her system. I wanted her as strong and pure as possible. In the hospital's labor room I was breathing hard and counting contractions and D. was watching *The Three Stooges* on television. "Shut up," he said as I panted. "You made me miss the punch line."

After Leigh's birth D. left to go to a party with some friends and told me he wasn't going to take me home from the hospital. "My friends only throw this party once a year and I'm not going to miss it," he said. "You're a grown-up, aren't you? Find your own ride home."

Dad was at church at choir rehearsal, and Mom wasn't feeling up to the drive, so I waited until rehearsal was over and my parents picked us up. D. didn't end up coming home until late the next day, so after my parents dropped us off I got undressed and took Leigh in bed with me. I nursed her and stroked her silky dark hair, and for the first time since Omma's death I spoke from the depths of my heart to another human being without fear or shame.

I told her how beautiful she was, how perfect and unique. I told her she was my darling daughter and the most amazing of all God's creations. I told her I would love her forever; I would willingly lay down my life for her. I thanked her for sharing her life with me. I told her that the bottomless void in my heart was filled with her arrival and that I'd waited all my life for the moment when she was in my arms.

Most of my talking was done when D. wasn't at home—he didn't want me to speak unless I was spoken to. But when Leigh and I were alone I talked to her constantly, telling her stories, reading her poetry, repeating over and over how much I loved her.

Leigh was incredibly beautiful to me. She had huge dark eyes and a dazzling smile. I was awed by her brilliance. At eighteen months her verbal skills were amazing: She could name just about every item in the house, and she knew the names of her favorite books and songs. She sang along with me when I danced with her around the house during the day and when I rocked her to sleep before her nap. By the time she was two she spoke in complete sentences; she read nearly anything by three.

I imagined that someday D. would die or leave us and we'd live together, just the two of us, and do whatever we wanted. No one would yell at us for playing too loudly or wasting time or not keeping the house immaculate.

And she would be the absolute queen of all she surveyed. I wanted her never to be sad, never to feel frustrated, never to be lonely. The love I felt for her shocked me with its intensity. I watched her for hours as she slept in her crib, lost in awe.

Once Leigh and I were home together, it was almost as if the world contained just the two of us. D. was gone most of the time. Mom didn't want to come over and help out because it was too tiring for her. I had no friends to come visiting, because D. didn't allow that. It was actually better that way. As far as I was concerned, that was the way it was supposed to be—mother and daughter creating a tiny island of peace in the midst of a hostile world.

....

I never cried during those years. Even when the terror and physical pain were intense, I remained outwardly calm. All the screaming went on inside and was usually directed at myself: "You're so ugly! You should have never been born; you were a huge mistake. No one will ever love you."

During my marriage, every slap and punch and kick were accompanied by a recording inside my head that played over and over: "That's what you deserve. That's what you deserve. That's what you deserve."

D. loved to water-ski, and we took the boat out just about every weekend. We were returning to shore one Saturday and I was sitting on the edge of the boat, leaning out to tie up at the dock. My left leg was dangling in the water between the boat and the dock. D. suddenly put the boat in reverse, slamming my leg for a split second before he turned off the engine.

When I felt the impact I was sure my leg had been severed, but I looked down and saw it was still there, although it had the oddest bend in it—as if someone had taken a paper doll and folded her leg in half the wrong way. Immediately it began turning a deep shade of indigo and swelling to impossible proportions. I had to go to the hospital, and D. was furious at me for ruining the weekend.

On the long walk from the boat dock to the car I alternately hopped and crawled, while D. walked on ahead. He never explained why he put the boat in reverse, and I never asked.

Chapter Thirteen

Shortly after Leigh's birth D. brought home a friend from work for dinner. D. couldn't leave her alone. He was charming and sweet and seductive to her, and I watched it all while I served dinner and cleaned the kitchen and gave Leigh her bath. Later, D. took the woman home. He didn't come home until the next morning.

We had a boat and a cabin by the river, and in the summer D. wanted to go there every Saturday. We had to get back in time for Sunday morning church, so I ended up driving home at 3:00 A.M. while D. slept in the backseat.

One day he offered a ride to a woman who was hitchhiking. I tilted the rearview mirror up so they weren't in view and kept my eyes straight ahead while I drove home, trying to concentrate on the road and shut out the sounds of them having sex in the backseat.

I got used to adultery. I was accustomed to the smell and telltale signs of it, and it caused me surprisingly little pain. I picked up the wineglasses on the bedroom floor and changed the sheets without saying a word or shedding a tear.

I knew D. loved sex. He just didn't love it with me.

D. said he could have sex with me only if he fantasized about someone else. He found the burn scars on my body revolting. He told me I was ugly. So he kept his eyes on a picture in *Penthouse* magazine while we were having sex; he never looked at me during those times. There was one other way: If I was in pain he became aroused.

....

I thought about death a lot—not just my own death, but D.'s as well. Divorce was unthinkable. It went against the word of God, and I couldn't imagine disappointing my parents like that and scandalizing the church. My only salvation, as far as I could see, was death.

At night, lying awake in bed with D. next to me, I thought of various scenarios in which I could kill him and get away with it. But they were always flawed, and I didn't want to get arrested. I was looking for a foolproof way. Only one time did the perfect opportunity present itself, and I had to let it go.

We were camping at the Grand Canyon, and D. and I had taken a hike to the rim. D. was a photographer, and he was standing right on the precipice, taking pictures. It was dusk. We were completely alone; there were bracken and pebbles underfoot. The ground was very unstable. D. had his back to me, and I thought: One push is all it would take. Then my marriage would be over, the misery would be ended, the physical and emotional abuse would stop. Leigh and I would be free.

Everyone would say how sad it was, but he shouldn't have been taking pictures so close to the edge.

Just as I was moving forward, I heard Leigh talking to me. I heard her wake up in the backpack. I could feel her feet kicking my ribs. She was facing forward. She would see. So I froze, and even though she was just six months old and probably wouldn't remember, I couldn't take that chance. I couldn't let my child watch a parent die.

D. turned around and saw the look on my face. He said, "What the hell's the matter with you?"

I didn't answer, and we walked down the trail, while Leigh sang her little baby songs.

With Leigh's birth, my view of death changed, even though my feelings about myself were the same. Now there was a reason for me to stay alive: I didn't want anyone else entrusted with my precious daughter's care.

I was terrified of the thought that D. might become her only parent, without me to protect her. Now that there was an imperative need for me to survive, the physical abuse took on a whole new dimension of fear. What if he didn't stop in time and he killed me? What would happen to Leigh? So I became even more docile and conciliatory, trying my best to ward off D.'s rages. I walked on eggshells, using whatever skills I could think of to keep him relatively calm.

I suffered most of my life with intense claustrophobia. D. knew it, and he used the knowledge skillfully. I'd sometimes awaken in the night to find him sitting heavily on my chest, knees locking my arms down against my sides, a pillow in his hands hovering a few inches above my face. When he saw I was awake he pushed the pillow over my face, just to the point where I was about to smother. Then he'd lift it up and I'd breathe frantically, seeing him smiling above me. Once I caught my breath, he'd repeat the game.

Once, when Mom asked me about a bruise on my face, I broached the subject of D.'s violence. I'd been afraid to bring it up before; I was ashamed of it and I felt it simply proved what I'd known all along—I was a failure as a human being and as a woman and I was completely disgusting.

It was obvious from the way Mom pleated the starched folds in her dress and looked over my head that she was extremely uncomfortable with the conversation, and I let it die away. Finally she cleared her throat and asked me if I'd asked the Lord for guidance. "Perhaps you're doing something that you shouldn't be doing," she said. "Why don't you pray about it and ask God to help you be a better wife?"

I should have known. Prayer, the unfailing panacea for any ill of flesh or spirit. There would be no help for me here.

Years after I left D., friends asked me why on earth I stayed so long. They were aghast that I didn't walk out after the first beating. And even after I explained they looked at me doubtfully, not completely convinced. I just laughed and said, "I guess you had to be there."

I wanted to leave, but the concept seemed as impossible as flying to the moon. Where would I go? Who would help me? I was completely alone. Everyone in town knew D.; everyone liked him. People thought I was damn lucky to have him—it's not like there were suitors lined up at the door. He was good-looking and respected and a community leader. No one would believe what went on when the door was closed. No one would believe me at all.

I couldn't disappoint my parents again. I couldn't let the church down. And here was the crux of the matter: I didn't deserve anything better. I was revolting, worth absolutely nothing. Of course he didn't kiss me or make love with me like normal people did. I wasn't normal. I was subhuman. I was ugly and disgusting. Of course he hurt me. I shouldn't even be alive. I was the cause of untold misery. I caused Omma's death. I disappointed my adoptive parents. I failed God.

No one would ever gaze into my eyes during sex and say my name and be flooded with love. And why should anyone? If I were a man, would I? Of course not. Given a choice, I believed, no one his right mind would choose me. I knew I wasn't the kind of woman that men fall in love with. And there was no question in my mind about why. I always understood. All I needed to do was look in the mirror.

I avoided mirrors as much as possible, and almost never let myself be caught in a photograph. But when I was forced to look at myself I was flooded with contempt. I saw a misshapen face, unruly hair, and ugliness that was beyond pity. I hated every aspect of my face and body: my quasi-Asian eyes, my wide cheekbones, and on down through each layer, to the skull beneath the skin.

When I was a child, I'd been punished for telling Mom and Dad that I wished I were married because I liked the way I smelled and felt and I'd like to share those things with my husband. This husband didn't want to see me, much less smell or touch me.

D. certainly wouldn't kiss me, and I only tried to kiss him once. We were sitting in front of the television after dinner, and the evening had been calm. I felt such relief that D. hadn't erupted into anger for several hours, and when he laughed aloud at something on the television I felt a surge of warmth and gratitude, and leaned forward impulsively and kissed his lips. He jerked his head back, then slammed his fist into my jaw. "Don't ever do that again," he told me. I never did.

....

For years after my divorce, I flinched when anyone moved unexpectedly toward my face. So quite often if I was dating someone and he reached his hand to my cheek, I'd jerk back and wince. Depending on how caught unaware I was, I might raise a hand to shield my face.

It was frustrating for the person I was with. They would sometimes become angry, because they saw my reaction as reflecting poorly on them, or they interpreted it to mean that I didn't trust them and I thought they would hurt me.

It was impossible for me to explain to their satisfaction or to mine why I reacted the way I did: how it was not a conscious act and that it was so hard for me to think that someone would reach toward my face lovingly. My reflexes expected to be slapped. It was just a response that built up over the years. It took my reflexes many years to learn that a hand moving toward my face now would end in a caress.

Having my face kissed is still to me thrilling beyond description. To yearn for so many years to be kissed and now to find that people are willing to kiss me—that it isn't a repugnant thing to them—is something I never get tired of. I never take it for granted. I still find a kiss the most amazing of gifts. It's a miracle to me that someone would intentionally and with desire move his face toward mine and put his mouth on my skin and take pleasure in doing so.

I think the fact that I longed for kisses for so many years made them so much sweeter when they finally arrived.

The impetus I needed to finally make the break from my marriage was Leigh. It was one thing to suffer myself—it seemed perfectly normal and right—but I couldn't let her suffer too. She trusted me to protect her, and she was the most precious thing on earth.

In an instant one night the decision was made. D.'s abuse that night took place in Leigh's room. She was a little over two years old then. If I made any noise, he said, she would wake and see what was happening. That was the only warning I needed to keep me silent.

I don't know why he chose Leigh's room that night—I think he was just getting bored with the routine abuse and wanted something new to spice things up. She was in her crib, wearing her yellow terry-cloth sleeper, the moonlight casting shadows from the slats across her beautiful face. I held on to the slats of her crib and bit my lips to keep from crying out, willing her to stay asleep. I was terrified that she would wake and sit up and look out through the slats and see what D. was doing. What if she peeked out between the slats and saw her mother being killed? At all costs, I had to keep that from happening.

As soon as he fell asleep I wrapped Leigh up in her blankets and slipped out the back door with her in my arms. I had nothing with me, no money, no clothes. I had rivulets of dried blood on my body and a panoply of old yellow bruises and fresh blue ones.

I walked barefoot through the brightly moonlit desert, carrying Leigh in my arms. I felt the most amazing sense of peace in the midst of danger, and I was in a strange daze, as if another scene from another time was being reenacted. I felt calmer and more serene than I had in years. There was a stillness that filled me, as if I were protected with my daughter in some safe place in the center of a maelstrom.

Leigh woke up and I sat down on a rock with her so she could play with some wildflowers, and we sang an old English madrigal she loved:

All 'round our nest, far as the eye can pass
Are golden kingcup fields with silver edge;
Where the cow-parsley skirts the hawthorn hedge.
'Tis visible silence; still as the hourglass.
Oh, clasp we to our hearts for deathless dower
This close-companioned, inarticulate hour;
When twofold silence was the song:
the Song of Love.

Leigh was accepting and unquestioning, and took pleasure in the walk and the moonlight and the song and the wildflowers. I walked through the night to my parents' house and knocked on the door. They let me in and didn't say too much when I told them I wanted a divorce.

I think they were both shocked by my condition, but they were well schooled in not noticing, so they averted their eyes; Mom told me to take a shower. After Leigh fell asleep I told them D. had abused me since the day we were married and I had decided to leave. They asked me to pray about it. "Have you asked the Lord's will in this matter?" Dad said. I lied and told them I had. I said the Lord wanted me to protect Leigh, and this was the only way to do it.

It wasn't until I told them of D.'s infidelity that they stopped lecturing. The Bible makes allowances for divorce if there's been adultery, Dad said, although the woman is not supposed to get married again. But that's the only allowance that's made. So my bruises meant nothing—I could chalk that up to the joy of being able to suffer with Christ—but adultery is a sin.

When D. came the next morning they tried to intercede on his behalf, but I felt—for the first time in my life—equal to anything. All the obsequiousness that had characterized me was simply gone. In a moment, without thought or effort, it was as if I were someone else. I was unmoved by D.'s pleas and threats and promises. I was unmoved by the thought of my parents' embarrassment at church or the disapproval of the town.

The time had come: my daughter and me, together and strong and safe, needing no one else.

Section

IV

....

The trees grow tall in the forest of my dreams.
They whisper and caress, intertwined by quiet streams.
Guide me, gentle light; silver moon on this dark night
While the leaves sing love songs to me.

The rain comes down in the forest of my dreams.
Through the mist I glimpse velvet, verdant green.
Wash away my tears, all the lost and lonely years
While the leaves sing love songs to me.

My heart's desire dwells in the forest of my dreams.
My soul moves with his form through the shadows of the trees.
The spirit of Pan in the body of a man;
And the leaves sing love songs to me.

....

Chapter Fourteen

I took one of the cars, a few pieces of furniture, Leigh's and my clothes, and some dishes with me when I left that marriage. D. kept the house, and the money. Since I was moving into a tiny place where we couldn't keep a pet, and D. didn't want her anymore, we had to give the dog to some neighbors.

From that moment on, Leigh and I built a life that was an American incarnation of my Korean life with Omma. We spent as much time as possible together. We played whenever we felt like it. We created a world for ourselves. When it got dark we piled books and pillows on the bed and cuddled up, reading and discussing and spinning make-believe stories and drinking peppermint sun tea until she fell asleep. Then I continued to read through the night, while her tiny dark head nestled against my shoulder.

Omma, who loved me just as passionately as I love my own daughter, wasn't able to run away with me, for whatever reason. With her death, I was completely abandoned. On the night I ran away with my daughter I felt an incredible exultation—we were tasting freedom, and we were tasting it together.

In a relative sense, my daughter and I were as poor as Omma and I had been, and we continued the legacy of turning poverty into a game. We went on treasure hunts until we scraped together enough loose change to buy a bag of rice. She'd emerge, shouting and triumphant, from rummaging behind the sofa cushions or under the car's floor mats, clutching some change. And, like me, it wasn't until she was much older that my daughter realized just how precarious her childhood's day-to-day existence had been.

Leigh and I stayed in the same town but moved into a $150-per-month apartment that stood in a row of shanties originally built for the migrant farm workers who labored in nearby date groves. It had one room that was partitioned off into a small living/sleeping area and an even smaller kitchen/bathroom.

It was reminiscent of the hut on the edge of the village where I lived with Omma—a squalid place for the very poor. We shared the apartment with a platoon of date palm beetles, overgrown specimens that scuttled round like armor-clad autocrats. When we pulled back the curtain in front of the tiny, stucco-walled shower stall they stayed put, clustered around the drain, and glared at us. They napped in the one row of cupboards that lined the living area wall and made their tracks around the blistered paint that peeled and dropped daily off the walls.

We had a mattress on the floor and a few pieces of furniture salvaged from our previous home. We decorated the place with wildflowers and long strands of field grasses that grew outside. Leigh drew pictures and we made frames for them out of colored paper I filched from work, then hung them on the wall.

I made paper dolls for her out of the same paper, and we used her crayons to make elaborate and fanciful clothes for them. Like Omma, I created a play town for my child and our fantasies became more vivid than reality.

Despite the fact that I had no college degree and no experience, I had managed to talk my way into a job as a reporter for a tiny weekly paper. The most appealing thing about the job was that I could take Leigh with me. She played underneath the desk while I answered the phone, and she accompanied me on assignment. I covered the local city council, the two schools in town, and the police and fire stations. I also was the paper's receptionist, ad taker, and typist. For my hybrid job I was paid $300 a month. On payday Leigh and I celebrated: We went grocery shopping, buying rice, whatever day-old bread was available, vegetables from the local roadside produce stand, and loose tea. We also treated ourselves to lemon Popsicles, which we ate outside at sunset, watching the tumbleweeds wheel across the road and waving to the Santa Fe train as it rumbled past.

As the month wore on and it neared the next payday, we usually ran out of money and food. Then it would be a scramble to find enough change to buy some rice or flour, out of which I made flat, unappetizing bread. But even the scramble was exciting. We went on "treasure hunts," looking for money. If we scraped together seventy-five cents, it was enough. We could get sufficient rice with that to see us through.

We were creative cooks, using whatever we could find to cobble a meal together. Our concoctions were sometimes surprisingly good; more often they were disgusting. But we ate them nevertheless, and made jokes about the food. We pretended we were Arctic explorers, down to our last meal. Nothing bad overwhelmed us, because everything became a game.

I had a battered old piano that a neighbor gave me, and often in the evenings Leigh sat on the bench beside me and we sang together. She rested her head on my lap and drifted off to sleep while I played and sang sweet Van Morrison songs:

She's as sweet as tupelo honey,
She's an angel of the first degree.

Leigh and I did pretty much whatever we felt like. Often that meant playing hooky from work and school. Occasionally I decided to leave work early. Once, for example, I picked Leigh up from school and told the school secretary she had a doctor's appointment. It was an August day, sunny and clear. Leigh was excited and eager and we both felt exhilarated.

I stopped at our apartment on the way to her school and changed into my bathing suit, then put my skirt and tank top over it. I brought her bathing suit along with me. So in the car, on the coast highway, Leigh hunkered down under a towel and changed into her bathing suit while we both giggled. We played all afternoon in the water until we were sunburned and sleepy and completely content. On the way home we stopped at Baskin-Robbins to get an ice cream cone and ate it in the car. Our faces and hands were sticky with ice cream and fudge and we made silly faces at each other.

When we got home we foraged around in the refrigerator, still scratchy with sand and still wearing our bathing suits. We didn't have a whole lot in it—some mashed potatoes and spaghetti sauce and peas—and none of it looked very appetizing to either of us. Leigh said that while it didn't look very good to eat, it would be lots of fun to finger-paint with. So we dragged it out of the refrigerator and dumped it all out on the kitchen floor. With our bathing suits on, we finger-painted with the food all over the clean white Formica floor, sliding around and laughing until our stomachs ached.

Friday nights were date nights. There was a drive-in movie theater in the town, so on Friday nights I piled blankets and pillows in the car and bundled Leigh up in her pajamas and pink bunny slippers and we stopped at Kentucky Fried Chicken, where we got the small box with three pieces of chicken, a roll, and some mashed potatoes and cole slaw. I brought along a Thermos of sun tea, and we cuddled up under the blankets and shared our little meal.

It wasn't the rice and kimchi and barley tea of my childhood, but the mealtime rituals were much the same: We shared the food—one bite for Leigh, one bite for me—and we saved the best tidbits for each other. We said the food tasted much better if the other one had taken the first bite, so we'd giggle and argue over who went first. We watched maybe an hour of whatever bad B-movie happened to be showing, before Leigh fell asleep. Once she was asleep I sat through the rest of the movie, or if it was too bad I drove straight home. I put her in bed, got in my nightgown and snuggled her into my arms, spooned behind her and kissed the top of her head. Like Omma, I made sure I was between my child and the door.

We went to sleep together and didn't feel poor or lonely at all. Sometimes we drowsily discussed the merits of the movie; sometimes we made up silly songs.

Like Omma, I wove stories for my daughter about her future: She'd live in a beautiful big city where all her dreams would come true. The stories were laced with the glorious passages we read together night after night; Coleridge and Shakespeare and C. S. Lewis and Roald Dahl all became parts of a lush, intoxicating make-believe tapestry. We took everything we read and made it uniquely our own: I recited poems to her from her infancy on, but incorporated her name into the works. Coleridge's "Kubla Khan," for example, was reworded to be her own property: "In Xanadu did Princess Leigh a stately pleasure-dome decree: Where Alph, the sacred river, ran through caverns measureless to man down to a sunless sea."

Whether in Korea or in America, the make-believe tapestry made life bearable.

....

As she got older, the necessity of togetherness for us continued. When she should have been playing with friends or pursuing her own interests, Leigh was with me. Separation anxiety was strong in us both. The only time we felt secure was when we were together.

While Leigh was still a preteen, we decided to become vegetarians. It was an easy decision for both of us. We believed strongly in the sanctity of all life, and in treating every living thing with kindness and respect. So when Leigh came home from school one day in tears and announced that she had seen a film about the horrible conditions inside slaughterhouses, it was a logical step for us to stop eating meat.

It was also pretty much the same way we'd been eating anyway, out of financial necessity. So we became vegans, with occasional lapses into dairy. We experimented with tofu and texturized vegetable protein and egg replacer, but mostly we stuck to the basics: rice, pasta, homemade bread, vegetables, and fruits.

I think we were the only vegetarians in town, and both of us got very tired of explaining for the umpteenth time why we didn't eat meat, poultry, or fish.

Being a vegetarian became, at that point in my life, the closest thing I had to religion. I was fervent about it. I identified with the animals that were raised solely for human consumption. I wept over the plight of chickens crammed in tiny, filthy cages, their beaks sawed off and their misery unheard.

People said things to me like "They're just animals. They're here for our use." I had a visceral reaction to that phrase, maybe because I was told countless times during my growing-up years that I was "just like an animal." I had suffered much of my life because I was considered less than human. Animals were suffering because they were less than human.

And it seemed to me that humans didn't have much to be proud of, if they treated other living things with such blind cruelty.

My parents, meanwhile, had accepted the divorce, but we didn't talk about it much. Leigh and I went to visit them every weekend, and we still attended their church—not because I believed, but because I wanted to keep the peace. They gave Leigh the same fundamentalist lectures they had always given me, but unlike me she didn't accept them.

"That's not nice," she'd pipe up when Dad said everyone without Christ would end up in hell. Leigh thought for herself, and never hesitated in voicing her opinion. As she got older she got more and more adamant. When she was four she took issue with one of Dad's sermons and told him about it. "I don't agree," she said. And when he asked her if she'd prayed about her attitude, her response was immediate. "I don't need to pray about it. I know what I think."

One of our first acts of emancipation was to move out of the desert. I was starving for green. I had never ceased to hate the desert, and I felt that much of my misery could be assuaged if I could simply walk outside and see a natural blade of grass or leafy tree.

In the desert where I grew up, there were cabins scattered in remote areas. You could scream and scream, and no one would hear you. Horrible things could take place behind those flimsy clapboard walls, and no rescuers would come. The cabins were miles from the main roads and miles from each other.

I still hate the desert. I never could see the austere beauty in it that others saw. To me it's a desolate place where nothing green and tender can grow. Any hopeful blade of grass or fragile plant withers in that merciless heat. Everything is scoured by the relentless sun and wind. People's skins grow dark and leathery. I think the desert dries out souls just like it does everything else.

Every night I heard the coyotes howling and the screams of some poor creature as they tore it to shreds. Quite often the victim was somebody's pet, a cat or dog that happened to be outside when the coyotes came down from the mountains on their nightly raids. Every night I put the pillow over my head, trying not to hear the death cries outside.

So with each succeeding job Leigh and I moved closer and closer to the Southern California coast. I attended college classes and worked my way up to larger newspapers. We moved into other apartments—still small, and still sparse, but without the date palm beetles inside or tumbleweeds outside.

Our second home was a tiny stone cabin on two dry, desolate acres on the outskirts of town. It was a step up from the shanty row, and since we'd felt claustrophobic being crammed between apartments, we were excited about our newfound privacy.

I didn't know until later how dangerous privacy can be.

I was working at my second newspaper, covering crime, seeing myself as some sort of small-town avenger of the innocent. I began work on a series of stories about malfeasance in the local sheriff's office, interviewing everyone I could find, digging for the truth. In the end, some of the people I was writing about lost their jobs and others were demoted.

Even so, I was on good terms with most of the cops in town, who knew that my coverage was fair and honest and who themselves wanted the bad apples tossed out of their department. Quite often a cop would cruise down the winding dirt road to our remote cabin to see if I wanted to go along on an accident or drug bust. Everyone knew where I lived.

One night I was awakened by the glare of headlights through the cabin's window, and my first thought was that perhaps there was a story in the making. Leigh was spending the night at a friend's house, and I was alone. When I opened the door to peer outside I saw one of the men I'd been writing about, and before I could react he was inside.

A half hour later he was gone.

My first call, for some reason, was to my editor. "I've been raped," I told him. "I think I'll be late to work in the morning." In less than an hour, he and his wife were at my door. I spent the rest of the night and into the morning at the hospital and the sheriff's station.

In the short time I'd been a police and court reporter I had covered a few rape trials, and had been horrified at the way the victims were treated on the witness stand. Right or wrong, I didn't want to go that route. So after several days of negotiating an agreement was reached: The man lost his law-enforcement job and entered counseling; I considered the case at an end.

A month later I realized I was pregnant. Abortion was the only option, but I didn't want anyone to know about it. I got an advance on my paycheck from my editor, drove into Los Angeles by myself on Saturday, had the abortion, and drove shakily back late that night, crying all the way home on Interstate 15.

I've struggled with a great deal of guilt over the entire sequence of events. I've chastised myself repeatedly for doing everything wrong: I shouldn't have opened the door without seeing clearly who was there; I shouldn't have lived in such a remote place where no one could hear my screams for help; I should have been courageous enough to take the case to court; was abortion really the only answer?

I've second-guessed myself countless times and I've grieved for the life that had to be cut short. But now I've stopped trying to decide if what I did was right or wrong.

Much of my fear about bringing the rape out in the open was that my private life would be exposed. If my life had been spotless by the standards of that society, perhaps I wouldn't have been so silent about the rape. But it wasn't. I couldn't have taken the witness stand and presented a virginal persona to the jury. I was ashamed.

We continued to live in that cabin throughout the next year. A couple of months later I was outside hanging clothes to dry when I suddenly slumped to the ground. It was about noon on a Saturday, Leigh was at her friend's house, and I had no idea what had happened. I wasn't in pain, but it felt as if my spinal column had melted away. I couldn't move my legs; I had no control over my lower body.

The clothesline was about a hundred feet from the house, and it took me the rest of the afternoon to drag myself back inside, using my arms and head to gain traction. When Leigh, who was eleven, came home I was lying on the kitchen floor because I wasn't able to reach the telephone on the kitchen counter.

She called an ambulance, and a few hours later a neurosurgeon told me I had to have immediate surgery to remove my fifth lumbar disc, which had slipped entirely out and was cutting off the nerves to my lower body. He gave me a litany of warnings: I might be paralyzed after the surgery, I might never walk again unaided, I might have to undergo a series of operations later to repair the damage.

I had the surgery and then went home to the little cabin for a long period of convalescence. During that time I had to remain either flat on my back or completely upright. Leigh did the cooking and cleaning and provided nearly around-the-clock nursing care for me, in her own unique style. She read aloud to me from Tolkien and Roald Dahl and Shel Silverstein and Shakespeare. She made tea for us and curled up on a bank of pillows, book in hand—the same way I had read to her a few years earlier.

Leigh was also my physical therapist. She led me in "toe-aerobics," where she pushed against my toes until she could feel some pressure back.

In a few weeks I was able to stand; several months later I was walking with a cane. Morning and evening, Leigh took me through a battery of exercises printed on a piece of paper that she found in the doctor's waiting room.

That was a frightening time for Leigh, as she tried her best to take care of me and make things as comfortable as she could. For a long while I could only crawl, and she would hear me moving in the night and get out of bed to check on me, then see me crawling down the hall toward the bathroom.

By the time a couple of years had passed I was pretty much back to normal most of the time, except for some loss of feeling in my right shin. I never knew what caused the back problems—the doctor said it could have been years of repeated beatings, but he couldn't tell for sure.

In the meantime, my editor and his wife brought us groceries every week, and he arranged it so that I got my regular paycheck rather than having to go on state disability.

....

The day we finally moved out of the desert we felt as if prison doors were opening.

We lived within walking distance of the beach and I was back to almost 100 percent mobility. Now we were in a bigger apartment with two bedrooms, a little patio, and a strip of grass where we planted tomatoes and flowers.

Reporters are notoriously low paid, and although I'd moved up to a larger newspaper I had to augment our income by giving piano lessons. I taught some of the neighborhood kids and a couple of adults I worked with, but not Leigh. I vividly remembered the painful, interminable piano lessons spent under Dad's tutelage.

If Leigh wanted to learn to play piano or guitar or zither or spoons or nothing, that was fine with me.

She was, like me, immersed in books. She also was a budding thespian, and our playtimes were rich with intricate fantasies and story lines and dialogue. Leigh was much the same kind of student I was—schoolwork was extremely easy for her and she lost interest quickly. She had little patience for people whose minds weren't as quick as hers; several times she got sent home with a detention slip because she had corrected her teacher's grammar or spelling or quotation.

Chapter Fifteen

The nightmares, which had been constant for me, began increasing in intensity when I hit my late twenties. I started walking in my sleep, something I'd never done before. I fell asleep usually around midnight and dreamed that I was locked inside a box, searching for an opening. As I walked around the inner circumference of the box in my dream, I physically left my bed and walked around my apartment. I usually awoke standing in front of a window, which I had opened in my sleep, leaning out gulping the cold night air.

Leigh often went looking for me

in the night and found me in some unlikely place, sometimes walking around outside blindly, sometimes curled in a fetal position on the floor. Often, she says, I would cry and speak to her in a mixture of Korean and English as she led me back to bed.

Since I thought I remembered no Korean other than a few basic words, I was amazed at what she told me. I wrote down some of the words, hoping the entire language eventually would come back to me.

I had never kept secrets from Leigh, and she knew nearly as much about my past as I did. She became increasingly insistent that I do two things: get help to deal with the immediate pain and do research to find out as much as possible about my childhood.

At around the same time, I entered an abyss of depression that was almost debilitating. Often I couldn't manage to get to work, and called in sick. On those days I sat in the living room, staring at the wall. The laundry piled up; the sink was filled with dirty dishes. If I went to work, it took every ounce of my strength and concentration to get through the day, and my work, of course, was barely acceptable.

I finally asked for help. The fantasies about suicide, which had always been present, were becoming my only daydreams and my only comfort. I fantasized about suicide in the way that some people fantasize about lovers. The thoughts were very explicit and very tender.

I knew exactly what I was going to wear, what I looked and smelled like, what the surroundings were. I would be dressed in white, with my hair braided and wrapped in a blue silk ribbon. My feet would be bare. I would be fresh and clean. I'd go into a forest and find a beautiful tree that I felt some spiritual connection with. I'd ask its permission, and when I felt the right moment come I'd hang myself from its holy branches.

I had the suicide fantasy mapped out to the smallest detail. I didn't want anyone just to stumble on my body, especially not a child. I didn't want to upset anyone who wasn't prepared for what they were about to see.

I planned to leave signposts to help law-enforcement people find me; I planned to leave a letter guiding sheriff's deputies and the coroner to my body. I planned to put up some warning signs just in case some unwary hiker happened along. I didn't want to upset anyone; I didn't want to traumatize anyone.

I knew exactly how I would dispose of my personal belongings. I'd leave my house clean so there would be no work left. I didn't want to inconvenience anyone. I just wanted to leave so badly. And yet I didn't want my daughter to lose her mother. So I was completely torn, and angry at being torn. And the one thing that I wanted—the one dream I had—I couldn't bring to fruition. I felt I was in a no-win situation. I felt there was no hope.

I knew that if I was going to stay alive, it couldn't be under these conditions.

Many of my nightmares were recurrent. I often dreamed of wandering through the house, looking for my mother. The rooms were empty and silent, and I ended up in the bathroom, where I opened the medicine cabinet and found her in a Mason jar, cut in tiny pieces.

I dreamed of a wooden coat tree covered in hats. I was afraid of the tree and yet fascinated with the various hats—some new and fancy, some tattered and greasy—hanging there. As I turned the hat tree around I came upon the disembodied head of a man. I recognized him immediately as the man I loved. His was not a face I'd ever seen before or one I knew from waking life, but I knew instinctively that I loved him dearly and he was my soul mate. I was afraid of him too, though. He asked me not to look at him because he felt disgusting and frightening, and I told him that to me he was the most beautiful and wonderful person in the world. I touched his face and kissed him over and over—his eyes, his mouth, his cheeks and forehead—and we both wept. I felt a surge of longing and tenderness and romantic love that I'd never felt in waking life.

Like him, I was afraid to show my face—or my soul—in all its nakedness. I was afraid of horrifying people. I longed to be seen and touched and kissed, even disembodied as I was. Like him, I surrounded myself with different hats and used them as protection. I was charming and funny in public, but I always felt lonely. I was kind and generous, but I always felt used. I was sympathetic and understanding, but I always felt angry.

I often dreamed of wandering through the church where I grew up, searching for little pink-frosted cupcakes. I looked in all the church cupboards and the Sunday school rooms, and finally I saw a plate of them hidden away in a janitor's closet. I was dying for one of them, wanting the sweetness and creaminess of them, but when I picked one up I saw that it was rotten and the underside was covered with maggots.

I often dreamed of being in my parents' house. Their toilet would begin to overflow, and a stream of feces and vile-smelling liquid would begin streaming out over the toilet seat and onto the floor. I had to clean it up, but it was like the Augean stables—no matter how hard I cleaned, it was still dirty. Even though I realized I'd never be able to win, I felt compelled to keep cleaning.

Many of my dreams contained animals, bound with chains and injured, dying slowly and agonizingly. Foxes, usually, or opossums. I'd often dream that I was lying in bed, my eyes shut tight. In the background I could hear someone say, "We'll have to sever her head so she can't see what's happened."

When I started trying to find healing—through therapy, through meditation, through finally talking about my life and reaching out for friends—I plodded on despite my firm belief that my soul was genetically flawed, that any spark of hope was doomed to disappointment. Like Blake, I believed there were some people who simply were without hope, and I was one of them:

Every night and every morn, some to misery are born.
Every morn and every night, some are born to sweet delight.
Some are born to sweet delight;
Some are born to endless night.

I had no doubt that I was born to endless night. And one of the reasons I was hesitant for a long time about really changing the way I looked at myself and the way I embraced the thought of death was because of an unspoken pact I made with Omma. Dreams of reuniting with my mother were accompanied by the belief that I needed to suffer as badly as she suffered. If she was willing to die, then I should be too.

Otherwise, I thought, the suffering of my lifetime had no meaning. My therapist relayed a famous quote to me: "Suffering without meaning equals despair." The meaning of the suffering, for me, was being linked with my mother.

As the excruciating process of trying to heal progressed, my recurring dreams shifted. I began having flying dreams again and quite often, and in them I was often searching for a child. Sometimes I'd find her, and swoop down and pick her up. She'd wrap her arms around my neck, I'd cradle her, and we'd fly off together. Sometimes she'd pull the skin over my chest apart and crawl inside, and the pain was intense.

Chapter Sixteen

Leigh's words:
*It is from our parents that we learn
whom to become; in their eyes we see
reflected our faces. The constancy of
their presence eases us, it gives us a
safe place from which we can observe
the world. My mother never had that
place. She was not given the luxury of
safety, and she spent years searching
for her reflection in someone or something. I had her, but she had no one,
and so I became her anchor as she
began to walk down the path of self-
discovery and realization. I was her
reflection, a small version of herself,
and a living chance to erase the pain
that she had felt in her childhood. In*

me, I think, she saw an opportunity to make right the half-remembered horrors and injustices that had haunted her all of her life. When I was very young she spent every moment worrying about my comfort and happiness, and although she could not shield me from all horror, she created for me a world that was safe and insulated. In spite of that, I can count on one hand the times in my childhood when I saw her truly laugh.

Through her generosity, her love, her affection, there was always sadness. I took it for granted and never thought to question that life was mostly a somber occasion. And it was not without struggle that I ever learned to think otherwise. There is no part of me that can blame her for the sadness. I cannot sit in judgment over a life that has seen such tragedy and pain. I could not ask for a more loving, more devoted mother. Nonetheless, I felt a tremendous responsibility to care for her. To shield her. And of course, in spite of my best efforts, I could not save her from the inevitable deluge of memories, or from the horror of healing.

As I entered my teenage years she began to enter her own period of awakening and self-discovery. Although those years are in many ways only shadows for her, for me every moment is as clear as the one I am experiencing now. At times the pain would be so great for her that she would drift away, taking whatever comfort she could in simply not being aware of the circumstances. Many times I asked her if it might be better to not go through the trauma of recovery. And many times she could not give me an answer.

I have begun to realize, looking back, that it was my exit from childhood that marked the beginning of her journey. She had always allowed herself to be swallowed completely by my helplessness, and in caring for me she forgot herself. When it was no longer necessary for her to devote every waking moment to me, her own thoughts and her own scars began to be insistent, coloring

185

every moment of her life, including, many times, her interactions with me.

It was not a quick process, but in the scope of a life, it was a short period of time between my childhood and the remembrance of hers, and the moment when mine came to an end.

Through it all I was never in the dark about what was happening at a particular moment. She would tell me thought to thought what was emerging in her mind, and although I understood little of it, it was those glimpses into her heart that saved me from feeling completely confused. Sometimes in the night she would talk to me. I would sit by her bed, and in a strange mixture of Korean and English, she would give me, and herself, clues to the things she had been through. I recall growing up with the knowledge of the orphanage and of mountains haunting me.

It is not difficult to see why she remembers most of all from that period the dreams. They were so vivid and so constant that they almost subsumed her waking life. Then when I was about fifteen, she began to walk in her sleep.

At first it was nothing to worry about; I would find her in the living room or in the kitchen in the middle of the night, and when I would question her she would seem confused and then soon go back to bed. Before long, the wanderings went farther, became more frequent, became more dangerous. As she remembered more and more of her past, her subconscious took her farther and farther from where I could protect her. She would walk into the backyard, or into the street, never having any conscious idea of what she was doing. Then I would find her, confused and crying, outside in the night. And I would talk to her, wrapping blankets around her shoulders, and she would come back inside, not knowing what she was looking for in the dark, but knowing that she hadn't found it.

....

I spent many years working as a newspaper reporter in Southern California, covering mainly police and courts. I loved my beat, and a big part of its appeal was the danger involved. I deliberately placed myself in situations that were life-threatening, without realizing my motivations.

My police scanner was always on, even when I went to bed. The sound of the codes and the dispatchers' voices and the static on the airwaves was comforting to me. Whenever anything newsworthy came across the scanner, I was awake immediately. I covered murders and gang wars and hostage situations and fires, and tried to get as close as I could to the action.

One night I went out to cover a gang fight and ended up in the middle of the melee, notebook in hand. I think that sometimes my naïveté saved me—people were often so bemused by my lack of caution that they shook their heads and took care of me. That night I got an interview with one of the gang leaders, who then told me he'd wait five minutes so I could get to safety.

Another time I covered a hostage situation and inched my way into the line of fire before being yanked back behind an angry but protective cop. The officers loved my boldness, though, even when they scolded me for it. I covered vice and was regularly issued a bulletproof vest when I went on graveyard shift ride-alongs.

All the time, I was zealous about what I believed my role was—a defender of the public's right to know and a guardian of the truth. I chose a profession that tapped into my deepest needs: the need to be heard, the need to speak the truth and be believed, the need to work for justice. I went from learning a new language to making that language my life's work. I went from feeling that I had no voice to writing words for thousands of people to read every day.

As a reporter, I had a fixation with people who were in need, especially if they were children, single mothers, or abused women.

I was light-years away from the woman I had been during my marriage, but I still remembered vividly how she felt and thought and behaved. When I would hear people criticize a domestic violence victim—"Why doesn't she just leave?"—I seethed. No one who hasn't been there can completely understand.

On one of my police ride-alongs, I met a woman who had been in an abusive marriage for nearly thirty years. A neighbor called the police because of the screams she heard, but when we got there the woman said everything was fine and she didn't want to press any charges. Her husband had left the house. The cop was impatient and brusque; the woman was apologetic and embarrassed. I stood in the background and watched her, thinking how easily I could have been in her place.

Before we left I went up to her and held out my hand, feeling helpless and heartbroken. My eyes were brimming with tears and I couldn't think of anything to say except "I'm sorry. I'm so sorry." I gave her my business card and said, "I don't want to do a story on you or anything like that. I've been in the situation you're in now and I just want to help in any way I can. Even if you just want to talk sometime or you need a ride somewhere or anything, please call me."

About a week later she did call, and we began a phone relationship that lasted for a couple of months.

She would never meet me anywhere; she said her husband didn't allow her to leave the house without his permission and she had to call when he was at work. I understood that perfectly. She told me she had never held a job and had only a high school diploma. She didn't think she could support herself, and she didn't even know how to open a checking account or get utilities turned on.

But above and beyond all the logistics was her core belief that she deserved nothing better. "You've seen me," she said. "I'm not young. I'm not pretty. I'm nothing. I don't blame him for not loving me. At least I have a place to live and food to eat. I'd probably end up homeless. It's too late for me."

I listened and listened, and tried to give her ideas where I could—the number of the abused women's shelter, some people I knew who could help get a new life started for her—and I marveled at whatever twist of fate had saved me from ending up like her. One day, though, she simply stopped calling.

Some of my choices made Leigh feel neglected and hurt. I brought people home from time to time whom I'd met out on a story—a mother and child who were homeless, an elderly woman who came into the newsroom with a hard-luck story, two orphans from a fatal car crash in which the parents were killed.

The two orphans were sisters, one two years old and the other four. They were Romanian immigrants whose parents had just recently come to this country. The two girls were strapped in their safety seats in the back of the car, and they escaped without injuries. But they were forced to see their parents' bodies crumpled in the front seat after a truck slammed into their compact car.

I became obsessed with those girls. I visited them in their foster home every day after the crash. I took them toys. I even asked about the possibility of adopting them.

I gave people whatever money I had if they were in need,

and the upshot was that sometimes I didn't have enough money to pay the bills or buy the things Leigh and I needed.

Helping others who were in dire straits allowed me to forget how poor we were, and also allowed me to focus whatever sorrow and compassion I could muster on someone else instead of myself.

Being a cop reporter meant I saw awful things on an almost daily basis. But now I was the observer, not the victim. I could watch and write and stay above the fray.

Because of the nature of my beat, I came face to face with death quite often, and I edged myself as close to it as possible. There was the time I covered a kidnapping and managed to grab the child who was being held hostage seconds after a police sharpshooter killed the suspect. I wanted to hold on to the child and not let him go. I wanted somehow to heal him, to give him some sense of safety or love, but I was powerless to do anything but write about it.

There was the time I held a prostitute in my arms as she died after being shot by an enraged client. I cradled her and looked into her eyes, thinking that perhaps I could convey something important to her: that she was of immeasurable value, that she didn't have to leave this life alone. I felt as if I had a magical power somehow to save people in their last few moments—even though I didn't know from what—if I just held them tenderly enough or looked deeply enough into their eyes.

Another time I went out to cover a car wreck and knelt by the dying woman who was pinned in the driver's seat, wrapping my sweater around her shoulders and talking to her as she took her last few breaths. She was a complete stranger, but in those seconds I felt like I knew her. "You're so precious," I told her.

"You're not alone. I love you. I care about you. I'm so honored to be here with you."

I don't know if anything I did had any effect on the people who were dying, but I needed to try—over and over—to ease someone's final journey. I needed to say good-bye in a way I never could with my own mother. It broke my heart to think of someone leaving this life feeling alone and unloved.

Chapter Seventeen

All the time I was running headlong into danger in my working life, I was constantly afraid.

My lifelong claustrophobia, for example, had deepened to such proportions that for years anything that threatened me with the loss of freedom was more terrifying than I could even contemplate.

For a long time I carried a steak knife in my car, hidden underneath the cup holder between the two front bucket seats. I carried it as a kind of security blanket—not ever to use on anybody else, but to use on myself in case I was ever mistakenly arrested for anything. I believed that if I was ever handcuffed and put in the back of a patrol car and taken to jail and locked in a cell, the terror would be so overwhelming that I would lose my mind. I would simply go crazy. I pictured it all so clearly. I'd begin to scream and hyperventilate and thrash and spiral into complete terror. I would rather die than experience that again.

To live locked up again was unthinkable. So I carried the knife—as unlikely as it was that I'd ever be arrested—because I knew that if I had to I could choose my moment and, in an instant, take two long, vertical slices down my forearm and one across my jugular. I would die before they had a chance to handcuff me, before they had a chance to lock me up again in a cage where I couldn't get out. I considered it a huge victory—and a frightening foray into the unknown—when I was finally able to throw away the knife and drive without it.

The fear for me of being immobilized, of being caged, has always been so intense and real that it overshadowed most other things in my life. It manifested itself as claustrophobia that made it impossible for me to fly in a plane, because those heavy doors are shut and there's no way out. I couldn't ride in the backseat of a two-door car. If I had access to a door handle, I knew that I could jump or roll out, and I felt a little more secure.

I couldn't ride in an elevator, because when those doors closed I was inside a cage again. So much of my life was tailored to keeping me out of situations that would trigger that terror. And I also despised myself for that weakness. I despised myself for not being able to fly in a plane. I despised myself for breaking out in a sweat and shaking uncontrollably if I had to ride in an elevator.

One time I was going to a job interview in a secure high-rise newspaper building. When I stepped into the lobby, all that was there was a reception desk and an elevator. I entered the elevator because I had no choice; there were no stairs available. But I didn't know you had to get a special key from the security guard to make the elevator move and send it up to the newsroom. So the elevator doors closed and it just stayed put.

I panicked. I was dressed up; I had on a suit and my makeup and hair were neat. But immediately I began to cry, so mascara ran down my cheeks. I began to perspire and shake. My heart was pounding painfully hard. I began banging on the elevator doors and screaming. The security guard opened the door and looked at me. Laconically he handed me the key and said, "You need this to get to the newsroom."

It seemed like an eternity that I was stuck in the elevator, but when the guard opened the door and I looked at the clock above the reception station, I had been in it only about three minutes.

....

In my early twenties I went to a city bookstore with a friend. In the poetry aisle I began leafing through books, as I always did, and I picked up a book by Edna St. Vincent Millay. Letting it fall open, I read, "What is my life to me? And what am I to life?" I burst into tears right in the middle of Barnes & Noble. There it was, the poem I read when I was ten years old, on that magical afternoon. There were the words that had stayed in my heart most of my life, the poem I had longed to find again and looked for repeatedly over the years. There, finally, was the poet who said exactly what I felt about death and loss and remembrance.

I had continued to write—in my daily job, in my private journal, in poetry—and the written word was of paramount importance to me. Reading about the pain and triumphs of others kept me from sinking into self-pity. Interviewing people every day who faced their own instances of hopelessness and despair kept me compassionate. And reading poets like Millay gave me hope.

Over the years my literary tastes evolved, but I still found myself speaking the lines of the writers I loved, as I had in seventh grade to Joe, who broke my heart. I still found the men in my life, on whatever level and at whatever period, unable to comprehend what I was saying, why the written word meant so much to me and why I was so disappointed that it meant nothing to them.

I'd steer the conversation to literature, and then recite, for instance, a Shakespearean sonnet such as "When, in disgrace with Fortune and men's eyes," or an Edna St. Vincent Millay poem. And usually, even though I wasn't aware of it except maybe on the edge of my consciousness, it was a test.

I'd decide to speak those lines and see what happened. I was always disappointed. Usually the man would look at me blankly and change the subject, or say "Oh, what's that?" and I'd tell him and he'd say, "Hmm. And you memorized it. Why?" It never lived up to my fantasy. What I wanted was for someone to feel the same way I felt about the lines.

That only happened once. I recited a snippet from a Michelangelo poem to a man I was dating, and he perked up and said, "That's right, I had forgotten Michelangelo wasn't just an artist but a poet as well." My heart leaped, and I said, "Yes, he was wonderful. I have a book of his poems if you'd like to see it." I handed him the book and he flipped through it and said, "Oh, and it has the Italian versions. I'm fluent in Italian." That bowled me over, even though I've always felt inferior around people who speak other languages or are well traveled. But anyway, I thought, "Maybe this is it. Maybe this man has the depth and romance and beauty of spirit that I've been looking for."

So he read the Italian out loud to me and translated it, and I was entranced. That was on our second date.

Between the second and third date, I had built up in my mind a complete fantasy about this man: that finally I had met a kindred spirit. He would be deep and romantic and passionate and sensual and faithful and sexually eager, and still sensitive and brilliant and funny—all the things I feared couldn't exist in one man. On our third date, we went out to dinner and he flirted with the waitress outrageously: commenting on her legs and on what a babe she was. He even told me he had picked his secretary because she was so gorgeous. So my little dream house of cards came tumbling down, and I didn't go out with him anymore.

....

I know that any therapist worth her license could explain why, needing reassurance so much, I've had relationships with men who hate to reassure. All the self-help books and all the good advice about learning to love myself and finding the reassurance within don't seem to get to the root of the longing: to be sure that someone in my life will stay with me. That if I let myself love another human being and let myself trust, I won't be abandoned. That I'll be safe. And that when I reach out, the person I love will still be there and will be reaching back toward me.

From time to time I found myself in a relationship of sorts, and each time I hoped against hope that he would be the one who would provide what I was searching for. Each time it failed.

With each experience I groped blindly in the darkness, looking for shadows that resembled love. But the real experience, the sum and substance of love, evaded me. I yearned for something that I couldn't even define. I thought of each man as a shadow, and I longed for the love in flesh incarnate: tender and passionate, pure and dirty, filled to the brim and running over. Unbridled intimacy.

I had the same sense of doomed romance that I think Omma had. She fell irrevocably in love, and the result was tragic. I absorbed that memory, and added to it with years of reading Shakespeare and Brontë and sad English poets.

A couple of years after my divorce I met a man at work who fell in love with me. I can recognize that now, but at the time I thought he had some serious psychological flaw that made him want me. Our desks faced each other in the newsroom, and from time to time I'd look up and see him watching me.

One night he came over to my house and we sat in the backyard, looking at the stars and talking. It was summertime, and I was wearing a low, square-necked sundress. The moon was glinting off my skin, and Mike leaned forward and gently ran his finger along my bare collarbone. "Your bones are so beautiful," he said. The words were like an electric shock—I'd always felt so ugly to my very core, down to the bone, and for him for see beauty in even my bones was stunning.

For a second I almost believed it.

We dated for about six months, until the day he asked me to marry him. Mike was a serious man, and he courted me with verve and persistence. He wrote songs and poems about me—lush, romantic things.

He brought me flowers and treated me with tenderness. He was also passionate and physical. I broke his heart. I was disgusted with him for loving me.

After Mike, I dated men who treated me more cavalierly. Anyone who started to get too serious was immediately suspect—I believed that if he was sincere about me, he was obviously a twisted freak; otherwise he was just playing some sadistic sort of game.

Many of my relationships were with married men. I never actually planned them that way, but they just seemed to happen. Married men didn't usually demand too much of me, and I didn't have to worry about whether they really loved me. I didn't fear rejection with them, because I knew the rules going in. Those relationships felt safe and nonthreatening, and they usually just peacefully dissolved without too much pain on either side.

Sometimes, though, things got complicated. A couple of times I played the role of understanding lover so well that the men I was with decided to leave their wives. The first time it happened, my lover simply showed up at my house one night, suitcase in hand, and announced he'd told his wife about us. I was stunned. She began calling me at home and at work, and between my anger at him for hurting her and my guilt at being a part of it, whatever we'd had fell apart pretty quickly.

I continued to choose men who would leave eventually, just like my father left Omma. I didn't believe real love was possible for the likes of me, and every time a relationship ended I had another chance to berate myself. "See? Nobody will ever stay with you. Did you really think this would be any different? You're pathetic and revolting."

....

In dating, of course, my Asian American features always loomed before me as yet another hurdle to finding love. A couple of years ago a neighbor I had chatted with a few times asked me if I'd like to meet her brother. "Oh, he'd just love you," she said. "He loves mixes."

"Mixes?" I asked. "You mean cake mixes? Drink mixes?"

"You know what I mean," she said, patting me on the arm. "Mixes. People like you."

Even though I was seething, I smiled back at her because I knew that in her own middle-America, small-minded way, she meant well.

I didn't date her brother, however.

Men were a kind of salve for me. Their attentions numbed, momentarily, the pain I lived with. But underneath the numbed surface the wound was growing and festering. I needed to stop numbing it and let it be out in the healing air.

All the while I avoided real attachments to avoid pain, and then felt life was an empty, vicious circle. I avoided pleasure, and then said life had none.

I tried to shame myself out of the longing. I tried berating myself. I reviled and ridiculed myself. The longing wouldn't go away. There's a line from a Nine Inch Nails song that ran through my head all the time: "I just want something I can never have." That, I thought, was the absolute truth.

Romantic love was such a mystery to me. I thought about it often: What did it feel like? What did it look like, taste like, smell like? What thoughts go through your mind when you know somebody is in love with you and you have that same passion? I couldn't imagine. I just knew I wanted it. And yet I was afraid of it too: It might be too wonderful and terrifying. Because everything we get in life, we lose eventually. Everything we have vanishes someday. If love were to arrive, the knowledge that someday it would leave would be devastating. Everyone dies. Life changes us. Experiences and circumstances change us. And love changes from rapture to revulsion—I'd seen it happen over and over.

I didn't know if anything would be worth that kind of pain and fear. If someone said "I love you" and I felt the same and I knew I could trust him, wouldn't I want to hold on to it so much that I'd live every moment in terror? I just didn't know, but of course, I knew I'd never have the chance to find out.

Chapter Eighteen

I've never had an easy time sleeping at night. If I slept three or four hours a night, I considered myself lucky. I went through my days desperately tired, but at night it was impossible for me to relax. I was hypervigilant; every sound woke me up.

I knew that awful things happened at night, and if I relaxed my guard, something would hurt me. The problem was that despite all my vigilance, awful things still happened.

Despite my staying alert in the basket as the twilight deepened, Omma was killed. Despite my watching the baby all night in the orphanage, he was dead the next morning. Despite trying to stay awake at night during my marriage, I'd awaken suddenly to find my husband pressing a pillow over my face. No matter how vigilant I've tried to be all my life, it's never been enough.

In those night watches, waiting for the sleep that eluded me and afraid of the nightmares that were inevitable, my one comfort was found in poetry, particularly Edna St. Vincent Millay's "Song of the Nations":

> *Out of*
> *Night and alarm*
> *Out of*
> *Darkness and dread,*
> *Out of old hate,*
> *Grudge and distrust,*
> *Sin and remorse,*
> *Passion and blindness;*
> *Shall come*
> *Dawn and the birds,*
> *Shall come*
> *Slacking of greed,*
> *Snapping of fear—*
> *Love shall fold warm like a cloak*
> *Round the shuddering earth*
> *Till the sound of its woe cease.*
> *After*
> *Terrible dreams,*
> *After*
> *Crying in sleep,*
> *Grief beyond thought,*
> *Twisting of hands,*

Tears from shut lids
Wetting the pillow;
Shall come
Sun on the wall,
Shall come
Sounds from the street,
Children at play—
Bubbles too big blown, and dreams
Filled too heavy with horror
Will burst and in mist fall.
Sing then,
You who were dumb,
Shout then
Into the dark;
Are we not one?
Are not our hearts
Hot from one fire,
And in one mold cast?
Out of
Night and alarm,
Out of
Terrible dreams,
Reach me your hand,
This is the meaning of all that we
Suffered in sleep—the white peace
Of the waking.

The process became for me to learn that vigilance, in and of itself, is not what saves us from tragedy. I've learned it wasn't my fault for relaxing my guard; I could never have prevented any of it.

Leigh's words:

I knew that my mother had frequent thoughts of suicide. In retro-spect, I'm not quite sure that I wouldn't have rather been kept in the dark about that for a while, but in a truly honest relationship one can't pick and choose what will be known and what will be kept a secret. I think that for my mother secrecy was evil, for in her own life it had wrought such pain, and the air of secrecy around her early years was felt in equal measure with shame. So in raising me she was vigilant to keep nothing secret.

I believe that children know far more than we realize they do, probably far more than we would like them to at times; and I was certainly able to see what was going on in my mother's life from a very young age. Part of me knew that my mother did not want to be alive.

That is almost as impossible to say as it was to feel.

I was a young teen when she sat me down one night and told me that there might come a time at which she simply couldn't hold on anymore. I knew enough of what she was going through to not have to ask what this meant. She told me that although she would miss me terribly, she might have to end her life and leave me some-day. She said that when (because there really was no "if ") this oc-curred, I would make it, and that it would in no way be my fault.

But then we made a pact that she would make it through my childhood, so that I would never be alone without a mother to care for me. The implication was that when I was older and better able to handle it, she would feel more free and be able to do what it was that she really wanted.

There is really no way to articulate what I felt at that moment, a mixture of terror, confusion, and anger that I should be the only link between my mother and life. There was really nothing I could do but say that I would understand and that I would not be angry.

I felt paralyzed but held on, knowing that even if she were to be gone the next day, I had to hold on to every moment like it was the last.

Although she had no intention of killing herself while I was still young, I didn't see how adulthood could change my feelings, and I always wondered if perhaps there were promises and pacts that could be broken. I think that I spent the next eight years or so awaiting the moment when she would no longer be able to cope.

When I was an adult we made a new pact: that she would never take her own life. It wasn't until then that I released the breath I had been holding for so many years.

....

When I was in my mid-thirties I began meditating. I knew nothing about meditation and had a tendency to mock what I thought of as New Age gibberish. But I was pretty much at the end of my tether. For some reason I was no longer able to ignore the misery of a lifetime, and it was slamming into me like a tidal wave.

I still thought about suicide all the time. I couldn't sleep at night, and when I would I'd sleepwalk. My best friend talked me into attending a seminar with her. I had never heard of the speakers, but I trusted my friend, so I went. I had little patience for others in the audience, though. I'd whisper my caustic observations to my friend: "Look at that guy. Why doesn't he lose the tie-dye? I bet he's got those stupid Deadhead teddy bears on his VW van too." I couldn't understand why everybody had to talk in that slow, mellow style, and I seemed to be the only one in the building wearing mascara and lipstick.

But once the seminar started, the critic within me quieted

down. When I got home I decided to give meditation a try, but on my own terms: I wasn't going to wear Birkenstocks, I wasn't going to act like a sedated zombie, and I wasn't going to take it too seriously.

I found out some amazing things. I had always struggled with intense panic when I tried to push away whatever feelings were haunting me. I found that if I just acknowledged the feelings, the panic abated. Grief and pain and loneliness were left. The sorrows of a lifetime. Ten thousand sorrows.

I tried to cover up those feelings with temporary balms, like relationships with men. But I realized the temporary balms eventually ate away at me and created their own acidic pain. The permanent balm seemed to be just letting the pain come to the surface where it could breathe and heal in its own way and time—not trying to cover it up and mask it and slather it over with something else.

I was also learning to live alone. Leigh was in her sophomore year at college and living away from home. Adjusting to life without my daughter, best friend, and anchor was terrifying. Both of us needed to find our own lives; we had been emotionally intertwined since her birth and were just now going through the normal separation adjustments that should have happened several years earlier.

With her departure, I was forced to face myself squarely and find another reason for my existence. I had always predicated any worth I had on Leigh: She was so brilliant; she was so beautiful; she was witty and complex and tempestuous—I felt my life was valid only because it had brought hers into the world. As she got older, that kind of adulation was hard for her to take. She felt enormous pressure not to disappoint me. She felt responsible for my happiness, indeed for my continued existence in this life.

....

At that point I was also ending a relationship that had marked a turning point in my life. For the first time I thought that perhaps I might be worth loving.

The man was a married colleague, and what started as long talks turned into a physical relationship. He was unhappy and dissatisfied, and I was a way for him to leave his wife and reassess his life.

That failed, benchmark relationship was a catalyst for feeling much deeper pain, and even while I was in the throes of it I realized that bigger issues were at stake. Shorn of all the hyperbole, it was pretty simple: He chose someone else. It came down to another rejection. But I let myself feel it and thus begin to feel all the years of accumulated rejection. I felt their weight and intensity and knew I was acknowledging, for the first time, a lifetime of pain.

We were together while he was married and while he was going through his divorce, but once it was final he told me he needed to date other people.

I was able, at times, to laugh at the irony of it: The only thing that had kept our shitty relationship going as long as it did was our shitty relationship. All we talked about was our relationship and its problems. One or the other of us was always in pain; one or the other of us was always asking why. One or the other of us was talking about what was wrong with the relationship.

The fact was that we had precious little else to talk about. If our relationship had been normal and satisfying, we'd have had nothing else to talk about. And if we'd had nothing else to talk about, it wouldn't have been normal and satisfying. We had no shared interests; we had no shared goals. We had nothing together except pain.

As soon as his need for me diminished, he withdrew. For much of our relationship he clutched at me like a drowning man, then he finally climbed on top of me to pull himself out of the water. And he never looked back to see if I was going under.

But when I grieved for him, I actually grieved for the first instance in my life that felt like romantic love. I wasn't grieving the loss of a person; I was grieving the loss of a birth. I had felt like I was finally in the real world.

....

By this time I had completely turned my back on Christianity, although I never told my parents—there was no point in hurting them. I still felt loathing toward anything that smacked of organized, fundamentalist religion, so I loved reading the Dalai Lama's words: "My religion is loving-kindness." I realized that meant loving-kindness to everyone in my life: past, present, and future; and that meant loving-kindness to myself—in my pain, in my jealousy, in my fear.

When I tentatively recited for the first time the "Om Mane Padme Hung" mantra, the reaction astounded me. I felt a sharp, cool tingling in my scalp. I felt for an instant as if I were going to rise off the floor—to have a flying dream while fully awake. Then I burst into tears. The reaction was so intense and visceral and spontaneous that I didn't know what to make of it. I could let it simply be what it was, without need to dissect or explain.

I don't know exactly what Omma chanted—I can't remember her words. But studying Buddhism made me feel closer to her and closer to the core of my own being. It was one way for me to reach peace with my past and discard the false personas that other people in my life had chosen for me.

I knew, and acknowledged the fact with fear and wonder,

that when chanting or meditating I had flashbacks of moments spent that way in Omma's presence. I would sit cross-legged on the floor, close my eyes, and begin to chant, and suddenly sense my surroundings profoundly change: The carpet beneath me would turn to dirt, the sounds of traffic outside would cease, the scent of Omma's incense and the lilt of her sweet voice would fill the air.

I wanted loving-kindness to become not only my religion but my way of life. I realized that breaking up with my lover was the best thing that could have happened. Had we stayed together my search for personal meaning would have been near impossible. I'd be fighting on a daily basis those old demons of jealousy, doubt, uncertainty, dissatisfaction, ennui. This way I could meet the pain head-on, shake its hand, and then let it go. I didn't have to be its roommate.

Nevertheless, I held on to a healthy dose of skepticism. It occurred to me that, taken too dogmatically, karma was akin to predestination. If you could dismiss someone because they weren't predestined—or chosen by God for salvation—you could also dismiss them because their suffering was karmic and therefore deserved.

But I believed that my pain over that failed relationship was karma at its basic level. I let my immediate emotions lead me to have an affair with a married man—an act that seriously wounded his wife. In years past my behavior had wounded other people, including myself. And now I was reaping the whirlwind. But I didn't want to continue my lifelong pattern of burying feelings and ignoring the truth.

I didn't know what to do, except just keep being aware of each moment of loneliness and loss, longing and sadness, hope and encouragement. I tried to accept whatever feeling came along without fear or clinging or panic. I saw more and more clearly that this is the human condition. Loss happens to everyone and will until the end of human relationships. What I struggled for was to feel mercy and tenderness for myself and for everyone else who had ever suffered or ever would do so.

I considered the possibility, for the first time in my life, that things could be okay. I believed that healing was just around the corner; wholeness was just a breath away. I was becoming dear to myself. And things were especially tough then: My job was hanging by a thread, there was no one in my life, I was lonely and afraid about the future.

I was in the uncharted territory of healing.

Through it all, I held on to one hope: The road might be rocky as hell, but I'd get there in the end. The destination was peace, fulfillment, love. That was a first—I'd never known before such things could exist for me. I started to believe in my own strength, and I reminded myself of what I'd survived so far. I told myself that this latest mess was a walk in the park by comparison.

My old daydreams of suicide started to be replaced with dreams of becoming a whole, healed person. I began to see that anything was possible.

For the first time in my life, I started to have moments of looking within myself and being awed and delighted by the possibilities.

I was learning to savor fragments of wonder. With Leigh's departure from home I moved into a tiny in-law unit in the basement of a house in the hills above town. The house was nestled up against the lovely mountains, and all around were pine and eucalyptus trees and flowering plants.

Soon after moving in I went for a ramble in the hills and found myself lost after about an hour. There was no real danger, because houses were scattered around and it was a balmy summer evening, but I felt the old familiar panic well up. I was tired and very thirsty and scared because I didn't know the way home.

Wandering down a footpath through some dense foliage, I saw a wild plum tree tucked in with the evergreens. I picked one of the dark purple plums and ate it slowly, savoring every bite and every drop of the incredibly sweet, fresh juice. In an instant, my thirst was gone, my tiredness had evaporated, and I had a stunning moment of clarity. The plum was perfect; the moment was perfect.

As I stood there, marveling at the experience and wanting to hold that kind of appreciation forever in my heart, a deer came out of the woods and began nuzzling at the plums that had dropped to the ground. The deer looked at me but continued to go about her business with the plums. I watched for a few minutes and then turned and instinctively headed in the right direction for home.

Omma said life is made up of ten thousand joys and ten thousand sorrows. I realized the plum, the deer, and the day could be counted as part of the ten thousand joys—and that every moment, if fully savored, could take its place there as well.

....

At the same time I began looking at pictures of myself as a child—pictures I'd kept hidden away for many years. I had always hated that child and felt contempt for her. Now I made a conscious effort to really see her. I learned to love the serious-faced girl in those pictures, who had lost her mother, lost the only security she had ever known, lived as a prisoner in an orphanage, and was then systematically abused through adulthood. I asked her forgiveness for my past coldness toward her and for abandoning her as everyone else had.

....

I began studying Buddhism in earnest, and felt a deep sense of homecoming. One very powerful teaching for me was that in all the world, there was no one more deserving of love than myself. That was the absolute antithesis of everything experience had taught me so far. I had spent all my life believing that in all the world, there was no one less deserving of love than myself. I told myself that I'd try to love myself every step of the way: through the job glitches; through the sad, scared, lonely moments; through the birth pains of finding myself.

One night I lit incense, made barley tea, and wrote my mother a letter:

My Omma.

I want to share with you the changes that are happening in my life. I've always thought I should suffer like you, because I wanted to be allied with you. I wanted to identify with you. But I see now that would be dishonoring your memory. I want you to have your wish. Your wish was that I be safe and protected. Since you're not here anymore to do that, I'll take over. I'll do this in honor of you; in loving memory of the most loving person in the world. I'll take up where you had to leave off. And that way we will always be allied. We'll truly be united. We'll be working for the same goal—the protection and happiness of the child you loved.

I wanted to be like you. I wanted to be close to you.

Now I see that this is the only way to do that. To be like you I have to treasure the daughter you gave birth to and died to save. And I will, my darling Omma. I will do my best to ensure her happiness, her freedom, and her wholeness. That's what you wanted, so that's what I'll do.

I love you so much. I miss you so much. I'm so lonely without you. But this way I feel your spirit working through me.

I had always felt like I was living inside a bubble. The outside world was visible but murky, and I was separated from everything by this invisible barrier. I wanted to reach outside it and become part of the real world, become a real person. But a black, oily film covered the bubble, holding it down and keeping me from breaking it open. When my view began to change, the world began to look different too—brighter, clearer, painfully sharp and in focus. It was both disconcerting and wonderful. I felt as if I were experiencing the birth pains of new physical and emotional feelings.

When I began looking for help, the changes weren't all pleasant. I became aware for the first time of the enormity of my anger and grief and jealousy, and it was frightening. I was terribly jealous of just about everyone and felt guilty about feeling so jealous. I had always covered up my feelings by seeming gregarious, extroverted, and confident. In the end, though, I always felt alone, unknown and unheard, and fraudulent.

The first step, for me, was simply to feel. It took a long time and enormous courage for me finally to be able just to relax into the fear, the pain, the fathomless abyss of despair. I pushed away feeling for so many years, trying to stay numb, trying to float above it all. But even to begin the long, tortuous journey of healing, I had to feel everything that came before.

I was afraid that if I really let myself sink into all those feelings, they'd engulf me and I'd drown in them. But that didn't happen. Amazingly, after the first terror had passed and I was still alive, I found that not only had I survived, I was finding unexpected comfort in simply relaxing into the pain.

For most of my adult life, whenever I looked through my adoption papers, I did so with my eyes emotionally averted. I read them, yes, but without letting the words sink in. Finally one day I pulled them out of their tattered folder and smoothed out the yellowed sheets and let myself really, truly read them: *Mother: unknown. Father: unknown. Date of birth: unknown.* I wrapped my arms around my chest and sobbed until I thought my heart would burst. I picked up the paper, with its coldly clinical description of that nameless, unwanted child, and kissed it: the line that read *Orphan: girl*; the line that read *Mother: unknown.*

Sometimes at night, drifting off to sleep, I'd whisper, "I love you. I love you." And I was never quite sure if I was saying that to an imaginary lover, or to the universe, or to myself, or to a dream, but it didn't really matter. Sometimes just to say the words aloud and hear them hanging in the air was enough.

Despite everything, I still hoped. Alone in bed in the middle of the night, I whispered aloud the same words of William Morris that I'd been whispering since my teens:

Love is enough: though the World be a-waning,
And the woods have no voice but the voice of complaining,
Though the sky be too dark for dim eyes to discover
The gold-cups and daisies fair blooming thereunder,
Though the hills be held shadows, and the sea a dark wonder,
And this day draw a veil over all deeds passed over,
Yet their hands shall not tremble, their feet shall not falter;

The void shall not weary, the fear shall not alter
These lips and these eyes of the loved and the lover.

....

Like many people, I tend to get frantic when I think I might be abandoned again. I do destructive things: I hold on too tightly to whoever is in my life at the moment; or I offer them a means of escape over and over again until they think I'm pushing them away. I'm so terrified of being left, and my core belief in that eventuality is so strong. When I realize how precious someone is to me, I give them every out I can think of. They're going to leave anyway, I reason, so I might as well feel the pain now instead of holding my breath waiting for it to strike in the future.

And all the time, I'm longing for them to stay with me, understand and forgive me, love me in the midst of my fear and despair. Only someone who has experienced abandonment can make sense of such senseless behavior. And I'm afraid of myself. I live on the lip of insanity, and there are times when I feel myself sliding into that dark maw. I'm terrified of what I might become and of how I might appear to the people I love. Would they recoil from me at the moment I need them the most?

I hate the word "issues." Everybody has "issues." I have abandonment "issues." I have a friend who pronounces it "isooze," and that makes it a little easier for me to say the word—it takes the portentousness out of it and cuts it down to size. But it still sucks. So I work over and over on the damn "isoo"—in my own roiling mind, in meditation, in therapy.

In looking for the strength to keep going, I wasn't able to think in terms of "God" or "higher power" or anything like that. I had come to the place where I didn't believe in anything even approaching a deity, and I was vitriolic in my hatred of anything that smacked of religion.

So when my therapist asked me to imagine a force or being that could confront what I feared, it seemed impossible—until I thought of the person I became during the flying dreams. I was strong, powerful, fearless, swooping at will over the earth. That image of myself became the closest thing to a "higher power" that I could imagine.

Letting go of my love affair with suicide was very difficult. I still think about suicide, even today, but not with the longing and romanticism that I once did. In many ways, losing my lust for suicide was like losing a lifelong lover.

I had "survivor guilt" as well, and dreaming of killing myself assuaged my guilt. The thought of suicide also reassured me that no one would ever leave me again—I'd be gone first and out of the reach of earthly pain, abandonment, and heartache.

....

I am always skeptical when I hear of Americans adopting children from other countries. Yes, many of these children are saved from horrific conditions and placed in loving homes. But I hope that the new parents remember their children are strangers in a strange land, and that they use every ounce of sensitivity and patience they possess.

No one, least of all a traumatized child, can make a culture jump at hyperspeed. They need to have their own cultures brought into their new homes and honored. They need to feel there's nothing wrong with them that must change before they can fit in. They need to be loved and respected just the way they are; they need to be heard.

The fear of not being heard has stayed with me my whole life. One of my recurring nightmares runs along these lines: I've been in an accident and I'm completely paralyzed. My mind is clear; I know exactly what's going on but I can't speak. No one looks into my eyes—in my dream I believe that if they did I'd be able to communicate somehow that way—but instead they talk about me and jostle me around and hurt me. I'm screaming inside, but nothing shows on the outside.

I've also spent my life saying what I think the person I'm with wants to hear. My adoptive parents gave me a clear message on that first day: We won't hear you unless you become like us; you have to talk our language if you want to communicate. So I tried to speak the other person's language. I picked up their mannerisms and jargon and agreed with just about anything they said.

Not being heard was so awful that I was willing to take on just about any persona for the sweetness of communication. I've been afraid to disagree with anyone, I've been afraid to speak my own mind. True, heart-to-heart communication is so sublime, and I had to learn to be true to my own heart to experience it.

In recent years I've tried to have even a tiny bit of authentic communication with my parents. They had their own evolution as the years went by, and some of the harshness that characterized them in my childhood began to relax. I never told them the depth of the scars I carry from their actions, nor how far away I've moved from their religion. But they have conceded that they made mistakes and that their interpretation of Christian parenting went perhaps a little too far.

They love me now. I know that for a certainty, even though they don't really know who I am. They tell me that they're proud of me—words I would have given anything to have heard in my childhood.

I love them too. I know they suffered in their own childhoods and they lived with their own demons. Given their beliefs and their rigid upbringings, I think they did the best they knew how. They simply didn't want me to go to hell.

During a recent visit with them Dad broke down in tears and told me he was sorry for many things during my childhood. "I was immature," he said. "I didn't know how to be a good father. I'm ashamed of the way I treated you."

The changes in Mom are the most remarkable. As she's gotten older she's gotten gentler. Her memory of my childhood is sweet and tender, and I don't try to challenge that. She sat at their dining room table as Leigh and I visited with them, and she pushed around baby carrots on her place mat. "Here," she said happily, handing each of us some carrots. "These are yummy." Leigh and I marveled about it later: Mom wouldn't even allow a milk carton on her table when I was growing up— she insisted milk be put into a pitcher and placed on the table. And here she was playing with carrots.

She sits without complaint, waiting for Dad to take care of her. She's delighted when I telephone and she calls me "darling." She reminisces about my adoption and childhood and says I was the best thing that ever happened to her. She tells me I was a beautiful child.

Chapter Nineteen

Korean mothers are amazing examples of uncomplaining self-sacrifice. They work so hard, taking care of their husbands, taking care of their children, and their patience is limitless. Omma was the epitome of that cultural phenomenon. She gave me the best of herself, and did so in circumstances that stagger my adult mind.

She had no friends or family. She received no support or even ordinary civility from any other adults. She had been abandoned by the man she loved, and she was left to care for a child that no one else would acknowledge. She performed backbreaking labor, day after day, and she lived in abject poverty.

She knew nothing would ever get better—there were no dreams to sustain her, there was no possibility of rescue.

Nevertheless, she made sure my life was as happy as she could make it. She smiled and sang with me; she stayed up at night and played with me when I know she must have been bone weary. She treated me with unfailing gentleness and affection.

Like the good Korean mother she was, she made sure I got the best of whatever food there was. She waited until I had enough rice before she ate, and the hottest and strongest tea was poured in my cup. She wrapped me up in what blankets we had and then used her body as extra protection for me against the cold. She humored and indulged me, and not once do I remember hearing her voice raised in anger. She never struck me. Her love was absolute.

....

People today ask me about my path to healing, and I'm never quite sure what to say.

I don't feel "healed." I feel stronger, certainly; I feel human and alive. I don't know if true healing can ever happen in this life. I hope it can, but there are many times when I still feel swept away into desolation and see no hope anywhere. There are still many times when I doubt that I'm capable of inspiring love.

And like everyone else, there are many times when I feel utterly alone and terrified.

Nevertheless, when I look at the world from the viewpoint of another person's soul, I feel an intense wave of compassion and tenderness and grief for the pain that they've suffered, and a longing to expunge that pain and bring them comfort and peace. I'm not able to do that for anyone else. Much of the time I'm not even able to do it for myself. We all struggle alone through the ten thousand joys and ten thousand sorrows of our lives.

But because we are ultimately alone, and because life is so hard, every moment of beauty, every belly laugh, and every kiss are powerful and precious. I'm intensely grateful for every fragile instant of contentment.

For me, the terror of being abandoned began the night my mother died. Lots of fears were born that night. But the abandonment mantra—"everyone I care about will leave me"— has chanted itself in every moment of my life. I go back to that night over and over, but each time I seem to learn something new.

It was a long time before I could acknowledge how angry I was with my mother for leaving me like that and for letting me see it. Why didn't she send me away? Why didn't she take me to an orphanage herself? Why did she position me in a place where she knew I'd see so clearly what happened?

I don't have answers, but I believe she did the best she could.

She was a product of a time and place that valued honor and valor, and she worked hard to instill both those qualities in her daughter. I believe she wanted me to be able to withstand anything. I believe she wanted me to accept that both of us were targets for persecution, and she knew I needed the kind of courage and unflinching strength that could be refined only in the fires of hell. I also believe she loved me more than her own life, and whatever bad decisions she made were done out of fear and ignorance, but always with love.

If I could talk to her today, face to face, the first thing I'd say would be "I forgive you." And then I'd tell her how much I love her. I love her. I love her.

Although it is not widely recognized or discussed, honor killing is not a practice that died with my mother. Hers was not an isolated tragedy.

Recently I spoke with a Korean man who expressed no surprise when I told him of my mother's death. "Yes," he said, "was it for a sexual shame?" His attitude was resigned. "I'm not saying it's right, but you have to understand. That's the way the culture is."

In the newsroom where I work, wire reports of honor killings are not infrequent. They occur not only in Korea but in Israel, in China, in Iran, in India, and in many other countries. We don't hear much about them, partly because they happen in places that are far from us and the limited scope of our thinking, but also because in such cases it is often reported that the women committed suicide. And many of the people in those countries accept honor killings as an unpleasant but time-honored part of their society. They simply aren't questioned.

We cannot know the numbers of women who have been murdered for cultural transgressions, but we can imagine that there have been countless other children who watched their mothers die and blamed themselves; other people who grew up feeling faceless, soulless, less than human.

There are countless other women whose lives were savagely cut short—beautiful, brilliant, simple, wild and timid, ordinary and spectacular—women you and I will never get to know, and the whole world is poorer because of it.

Chapter Twenty

I've always dreamed about the night
Omma died, but as I've gotten older
the dreams have changed. Now
there's some comfort to be found.

I can go into that room and cut
the rope and take the noose from
around her neck and cradle her in
my arms. And kiss her poor blue
face until it turns that beautiful
blush-tinted porcelain and rock her
the way she rocked me so many
times. And close her wide-open eyes
and sing her to sleep.

Oh God, I miss her so much.

And in that same dream I can
step into the room as an adult and
pick up that terrified, bloodied child

and press her to my heart until my chest dissolves and she melts inside. I can tell her she'll never be alone again. I can tell her it's not her fault that her Omma is dead.

I can tell her she was worth saving.

That night, and this night, are like tiny tiles in the huge, multicolored mosaic of life. They're like fleeting shadows of a dream. I look out my window and see the reality: This life is like the dense fog that swirls around my deck in the morning—it looks real and solid, it takes on forms and shape. But when the sun warms it enough it vanishes without a trace.

Maybe this life is like that. Maybe this pain is like that. Fears and hopes and dreams and sorrows all will dissolve like the fog that they are, and what will be left is the light and warmth of my deepest self or soul or whatever it might be.

I want true love in this life, and true contentment and peace. But maybe the only way I can find those things is to let go of the belief that this life is my reality.

....

Exquisite courtesy
That you should see me
Immeasurable grace
For you to believe
That I, the faceless child of darkness
Could enter into hallowed halls of love.
Could touch, and find no shame in touching
Could hope, and find hope not in vain.
A peace beyond my understanding
Has fallen on my head like gentle rain.

....

E *pilogue*

Not too long ago I went to a Korean restaurant in San Francisco with a friend. We ordered a whole bunch of different kinds of kimchi, and we had rice and tea. About halfway through our meal, a Korean family came in: parents, two children, a grandmother. They'd obviously come from something fun—the kids were carrying balloons and had that grubby look of a day spent playing outdoors. The adults were laughing and affectionate with the children; the kids were demanding certain dishes in the supremely confident way children have when they know they're dearly loved.

I watched them, sitting across the room, and blinked away tears. I ate my kimchi and stared as they giggled and shared a feast of different foods. I wanted so badly to join them. I wanted to walk over and see their smiles include me; I wanted to become a part of that close, inviolate circle of family.

As we were leaving, three girls walked past us, chatting happily as they headed toward the restaurant. They were young friends, probably no more than sixteen, excited to be out together. The first two were talking and swept past me, but the third moved more slowly. We made eye contact and I smiled at her, loving her just because she was a young Korean girl, looking much as I had once looked, and seeming a little lost. She smiled back, shyly, then bowed to me. Startled, I bowed in return, tears filling my eyes. It was as if someone had given me a gift I'd waited for my entire life. For the first time, a Korean had looked at me not with scorn or even curiosity, but as someone to acknowledge and respect. I was accepted, and it made me want to shout with joy and press her to my heart.

The girl outside the restaurant had no idea what a profound effect her simple act of courtesy had on me. In Korean culture, the bow is everything. The person of least importance bows first as a sign of respect. The greater the respect, the deeper the bow. Never in my life had anyone, except for my mother, bowed to me. I bowed to her, as I'd bowed so many times to Omma, and was engulfed in a wave of love and grief.

Everything is possible, Omma told me. She believed that someday I'd be a person, and people would smile at me and bow to me and look in my eyes. She believed that someday her child's life would be of value.

Now her child believes it too.